LESSONS LEARNED

William G. Bowen

LESSONS LEARNED

Reflections of a University President

PRINCETON UNIVERSITY PRESS

Princeton and Oxford

Published by Princeton University Press, 41 William Street,

Princeton, New Jersey 08540

In the United Kingdom: Princeton University Press, 6 Oxford Street,

Woodstock, Oxfordshire OX20 1TW

press.princeton.edu

Library of Congress Cataloging-in-Publication Data

Bowen, William G.

   Lessons learned : reflections of a university president / William G. Bowen.

     p. cm.

   Includes bibliographical references and index.

   ISBN 978-0-691-14962-2 (hardcover : alk. paper)   1. Universities and colleges—

Administration.   2. Educational leadership—United States.   3. Education, Higher.

I. Title.

   LB2336.B68 2011

   378.1'11—dc22

   [B]

2010033781

British Library Cataloging-in-Publication Data is available

This book has been composed in Minion Pro with ITC Kabel

Printed on acid-free paper. ∞

Printed in the United States of America

10 9 8 7 6 5 4 3 2 1

To four lifelong friends

who taught me so many of the lessons

recounted in this book:

Paul Benacerraf,

Mary Ellen Bowen,

Stanley Kelley Jr.,

Neil L. Rudenstine

CONTENTS

ONE

Preamble and Context

Hard as it is even for me to believe, I have lived in and around presidents' offices for more than forty years. Much of that time (1967–1988) was spent as provost and then as president of Princeton University. Those years in Nassau Hall, the last sixteen in the president's office, were often tumultuous, almost always instructive, and rich in associations as well as experiences. The Vietnam War provoked a sweeping and highly productive reexamination of principles of governance that remain highly relevant; the war also raised probing questions about the role of the university in society. The civil rights movement added to the sense of urgency so many of us felt as we tried to alter the university's persona in fundamental ways while retaining those elements of its character that remain basic to the intellectual power of the place. Then, there were more locally driven debates over issues such as coeducation and how to build faculty strength (especially in the life sciences) in the face of high inflation, high unemployment, escalating energy costs, and depressed stock prices. It was a stimulating setting for someone learning, as I was, about life in a president's office.

During those same years, I served as a trustee of Denison University in Ohio, where I had been an undergraduate, and thus had the opportunity to see the somewhat different pressures that beat upon the president of a small liberal arts college. After leaving Princeton, I went to the Andrew W.

Mellon Foundation, which placed heavy emphasis on working with the presidents and provosts of leading colleges and universities. These new associations provided opportunities of yet another kind to see how different presidents led their institutions as they addressed myriad problems that were frequently generic.

I have often been asked what (if anything!) I learned from these experiences. This book attempts to answer that question. It is not a memoir and not a history. Rather, it is a series of reflections on lessons learned through confronting challenges that present themselves to almost every president—including structuring relations with trustees, recruiting able colleagues (and also securing resignations when necessary), managing an effective tenure process, setting academic priorities and then raising the money needed to give life to the most important ones, budgeting wisely in order to ensure the institution's long-term financial viability, reconciling the need to be orderly and even somewhat bureaucratic ("business-like") with the need to respect the special character and climate of the academy, creating an open and inclusive learning environment for students from diverse backgrounds, handling dissent and maintaining the openness of the campus to all points of view, protecting institutional integrity, balancing internal and external pressures on an unforgiving schedule, and, finally, deciding when—and how—to leave.

Nice as it is to get things right, some of the most compelling lessons I learned grew out of mistakes that I made. One characteristic of "lessons learned the hard way" is that a number of them involved a failure on my part to look closely enough at real evidence (pertaining to admissions, for example). I sometimes relied too much on what I simply assumed to be reality and succumbed to the temptation to believe what I wanted to believe.

I want next to acknowledge that, as Hanna Gray, a former president of both Yale and University of Chicago, wisely observed in commenting on a draft of the manuscript, what I refer to as "lessons learned" are sometimes more like "truths confirmed." Moreover, some of these "truths" seem obvious—*are* obvious—when stated abstractly and removed from the often-wrenching contexts in which they manifested themselves. My tendency to look back on situations with the wonderful clarity that hindsight gives all of us may make judgments sound easier and less tangled than they often were, given the "real-time" settings in which they were embedded—settings that were ripe with difficult trade-offs, tricky currents and crosscurrents. In short, the reader is warned that at times I may have violated, or come close to violating, one of my favorite Einstein aphorisms: "Everything should be made as simple as possible, but not more so."

In discussing "lessons learned," I will assume that the reader is familiar with the basic characteristics of both research universities and liberal arts colleges. It is not my purpose to discuss such topics as how the admissions process works or why academic tenure exists.[1] Nor do I provide a literature review or a systematic account of how this country's system of higher education has evolved. Instead, I use specific events and stories to illustrate basic points. But I resist speculating about challenges not yet experienced (at least by me). Thus, important as it is for all of higher education to adjust effectively to the severe fiscal constraints associated with the 2008–2009 recession and the slow recovery from it, that is a story for another day.

Since much of what I learned is based on experiences I had in and around the president's office at Princeton, there are, unavoidably, many Princeton references. At first I thought that this might be a serious problem—and it may be, for some readers. But the many commentators on early drafts of the manuscript (who are listed in the acknowledgments at the end of the book and often cited in the pages that follow) were nearly unanimous in arguing that it is a positive, not a negative, that much of the argument of the book is rooted in specific occurrences at a "known" place. Thanks to the contributions of many of these same commentators (including nineteen who were or are presidents of colleges and universities), I have included references to happenings elsewhere, and to lessons others have learned in different settings. Nonetheless, the book remains

---

[1] Henry Rosovsky provides a thoughtful discussion of most basic features of research universities in *The University: An Owner's Manual* (New York: W. W. Norton, 1991). I know of no comparable book on liberal arts colleges, but *Daedalus* (Winter 1999) published a useful collection of essays on these institutions: Steven Koblik and Stephen R. Graubard, eds., *Distinctively American: The Residential Liberal Arts Colleges* (New Brunswick, NJ: Transaction Publishers, 2000). Donald Kennedy, former president of Stanford, is the author of *Academic Duty* (Cambridge: Harvard University Press, 1997), which treats some of the same issues discussed here (and others) mainly from the perspective of faculty duties. Although I too talk at some length about the faculty, my emphasis is on the role of the president.

more "Princeton-centric" than I had originally intended it to be, and the particular characteristics of Princeton have unquestionably shaped my thinking. That being the case, I provide here a capsule description of Princeton so that readers will have that context in mind.

In brief, Princeton is a wealthy, private, research university of high standing with a long history. It is located in a largely affluent suburban community that is home to a number of highly educated people associated with knowledge-intensive institutions such as ETS (Educational Testing Service) and the Institute for Advanced Study, as well as Princeton, Rutgers, and other colleges and secondary schools. The university is residential, operates at a relatively small scale, and is highly selective at both undergraduate and graduate levels. The undergraduate college was all male until it became coeducational in 1969—a change that occurred a few years earlier at the graduate level. It has a famously loyal (some would say "fanatically loyal") alumni body.

Compared with other research universities, Princeton offers a limited range of graduate and professional programs. It is basically an arts and sciences university that also has programs in engineering and applied science, architecture and planning, and public and international affairs. For reasons that I discuss in chapter 6, it has none of the mainline professional schools (law, business, medicine, education) that are found in most research universities. An important organizational consequence is that Princeton has a single faculty, is highly centralized, and its president and provost do not have to deal with the innumerable complications present in more complex settings. The obverse side of this coin is that Princeton lacks the advantages that go with having professional schools that are linked closely to programs in the arts and sciences.

Princeton is without question a highly privileged place, as rich in resources as it is consciously limited in its organizational reach, and some policies that worked at Princeton would be much more difficult to put in place at institutions without Princeton's advantages. Still, I think that many of the propositions I discuss are transferable across a wide range of institutions, including those that are less affluent and less selective. Some also apply to foundations and other nonprofit institutions.

It is well to recognize explicitly that each president has individual strengths and weaknesses, and individual likes and dislikes, that must be taken into account in deciding how to lead and manage. Even within a given institutional context, there is no "one size fits all" when it comes to prescribing rules of the road for a president. Leadership styles will—and should—vary. The propositions in this book inevitably reflect my own proclivities and may or may not make sense for others.

Finally, it may be helpful if I make a few introductory comments about the culture and core values of academia in general. As everyone who has worked in a college or university knows, these institutions are less hierarchical than businesses and less "top-down" than many other non-profits and most governmental entities. But they are certainly not "democratic"—nor should they be. Although there are many differences across the landscape of higher education, shared governance models of one kind or another are found nearly everywhere, with heavy faculty involvement in many aspects of university life, especially academic aspects. Trustees (regents)[2] have the ultimate authority in all areas, but many aspects of decision-making and most tasks related to "execution" are delegated by the trustees to the president. The president in turn delegates some powers to other administrative officers and to faculty—who in some cases may then make more limited delegations of authority regarding campus life to student groups. Commentators on university governance have often noted that this multifaceted, layered system works tolerably well because most trustees understand that they would be foolish to exercise all of the authority that they possess.

Things generally get done through a combination of extensive consultation, much persuasion, carefully constructed incentives, and some sanctions—rarely by straightforward "commands," though of course presidents and others with executive authority must make decisions and take responsibility for them. This contemporary model stands in contrast to the more authoritarian model of earlier days.[3] It relies on both trustee

[2] Whenever I write "trustees," I mean to include "regents" as well.
[3] See Jonathan Cole, *The Great American University* (New York: Public Affairs, 2010), 66ff., for a discussion of the evolution of decision-making authority in research universities.

restraint and a general—though far from universal—understanding and acceptance of governing conventions by faculty, staff, students, alumni, and society at large.

Shared governance works for a second reason: the core values of academic communities, which lead to implicit "institutional rules," are generally understood and embraced by the key parties. The missions of institutions of higher education—to transmit inherited knowledge and simultaneously to build on what is known and to correct the errors of the past—are so deeply ingrained that they almost go without saying. Aggressive pursuit of new insights, collection of new evidence, and preparation for the ever-present possibility of being wrong all condition how members of campus communities relate to each other—as does the emphasis placed on the need for individuals to think for themselves. There are of course definite differences of opinion (thank heavens), and sometimes heated clashes over curricular content as well as over assumptions underlying research models, never mind issues of public policy. But these clashes occur within a framework marked by wide acceptance of implicit institutional rules that are rooted in a strong tradition of tolerance for different points of view. Commitment to some version of the idea of shared governance is a thread that runs through the academy. But this shared commitment to core values is rarely, if ever, determinative. There is plenty of opportunity to disagree on important matters—and to get things wrong!

TWO

Governing

At the end of the day, the president is responsible for producing good results in shared governance settings that must seem byzantine to many, inside as well as outside the academy—because in some ways they are! A president's chances of succeeding in such settings are directly related to the specific governance structure within which he or she operates. Much variation in structures and procedures notwithstanding, there is one absolutely key characteristic of any well-functioning academic community: there must be widespread understanding, certainly among trustees and key faculty members, of how responsibility and influence are shared—and reasonably widespread acceptance throughout the campus community of the legitimacy of the governing conventions. In easy times, none of this may matter much. But when difficulties arise, the absence of a shared sense of how things are expected to work can be problematic. It is highly desirable that a good structure be in place ahead of a crisis. In troubled times, energy should not be wasted fixing things that should have been fixed earlier—when it would also have been easier to fix them.[1]

[1] For a good discussion of this key point in the context of a university struggling to reform governance structures during still more contentious times than those experienced at Princeton, see Richard W. Lyman, *Stanford in Turmoil* (Stanford: Stanford University Press, 2009). President

The Trustees and the Resident Campus Community

The experiences on many campuses during the late 1960s continue to provide a textbook demonstration of the importance of good governance principles. Protests over the Vietnam War and related issues such as draft counseling often combined with debates over other policies (such as rules restricting the hours that members of the opposite sex were allowed to be in dormitories) to provoke serious challenges to the ways in which colleges and universities were governed. In the Princeton case, a major demonstration in early May 1968 (a week after Columbia was essentially closed down) focused not just on particular grievances but on what the demonstrators asserted was a need to "determine a way of restructuring the decision-making apparatus of the University."[2]

Those of us seeking to maintain some semblance of order and civil discourse—which was anything but easy in those days—had to agree that a serious reexamination of principles of governance was, if anything, overdue. Although there were of course a charter and trustee and faculty by-laws, there was no broader statement of propositions about governance to which people could refer—and to which they could object, if they were so inclined. Assumptions about roles were just "understood" (or not). Fortunately, Princeton's president at the time, Robert Goheen, had the good judgment to agree on the spot to work with faculty and students to constitute a Special Committee on the Structure of the University. We were able to persuade an extraordinarily talented, widely respected, and

---

Lyman emphasizes "the difficulty in creating new institutions, particularly under conditions of maximum stress and polarized opinion" (156).

[2] See p. 2 of the introduction to "The Governing of Princeton University: Final Report of the Special Committee on the Structure of the University" (hereafter the Kelley Committee Report), April 1970. This report remains the best analysis of university governance known to me, and its full text is available on the Princeton University Press Web site: http://diglib.princeton.edu/ead/getEad?id=ark:/88435/w37636770. The report is especially good in analyzing carefully the reasons we have trustees (and regents). Anyone who questions the contemporary relevance of these issues should read accounts of the protests in California in 2009 growing out of the extraordinary cutbacks in public support for that state's educational system. See, for example, Tad Friend, "Letter from California: Protest Studies," *New Yorker*, January 4, 2010, 22ff. At one meeting, police had to clear a room of protestors who were chanting, "Whose university? Our university." The chants were indistinguishable from those we heard in front of Nassau Hall in May 1968.

shrewd professor of politics, Stanley Kelley Jr., to chair this committee. The creation of the "Kelley Committee" was endorsed by the trustees, and it began its work more or less immediately. People with complaints and ideas for reform now had an established "place to go."

Recognizing the need for speed, the committee issued a highly influential "Interim Report" in mid-November 1968, less than six months after its inception; specific recommendations in May 1969; and a "Final Report" in April 1970. The work of this committee had a number of important consequences that I discuss at appropriate places in this book. At the most general level, it recognized that students as well as faculty and administrators had contributions to make and that it would be advantageous to provide established ways for the various campus constituencies to meet together. It also brought home the truth that deeply held views by members of the campus community have to be taken into account by trustees, even as they could not be allowed, in and of themselves, to dictate outcomes.

More specifically, and most directly relevant here, the trustees were encouraged by the committee to adopt a formal "Statement of Policy on Delegation of Authority." This 1969 statement both codified a number of long-standing practices and set forth a well-reasoned "philosophy of governance" that gained widespread support on the campus. It assured the resident university community that the trustees intended to continue to delegate much of their authority to act in the ways spelled out in the document. The statement also explained that the trustees exercise their duties in three main ways: (1) *general review* (of faculty appointments, curricular matters, admissions, and so on) with particular attention paid to "the integrity and efficiency of the procedures followed," as well as to the quality of outcomes; (2) *prior review* (of major changes in policy, any substantial new claims on funds, and budgetary decisions before final decisions or commitments are made); and (3) *authority directly exercised* (especially in the management of the university's endowment). It was understood that any matters not explicitly delegated remained the responsibility of the trustees, and that the trustees "could not consign to any other parties their final responsibility under the law and the terms of the Princeton Charter." As Ron Daniel of McKinsey & Company, an experienced member of the governing boards at Harvard, Wesleyan, and Brandeis, emphasizes: "Responsibility can NEVER be delegated. Only authority can be delegated."

The 1969 statement has been reviewed and reaffirmed periodically by the trustees and has been amended in only the most minor ways. For over four decades now, the clarifications and assurances provided by this document have proven to be valuable in providing an organizational framework that encourages discussion to be directed to the *substance* of issues, with minimum wheel-spinning and unproductive argument over where authority rests. It remains a centerpiece of the orientation process for new trustees each year. There is much to be said for having a document of this kind as a ready reference and framework for decision-making.[3]

In addition to being responsible for advancing the interests of the university overall, trustees have a particular obligation to think about the long-term effects of decisions. Of all the groups involved in university governance, trustees should have the longest time horizon. Students understandably want everything to happen "now," faculty members are naturally concerned primarily about the health of the university when they are at the center of it (and about their own requirements), and administrators want to succeed on "their watch." In thinking about the harvesting of returns from the endowment, for example, campus groups can be tempted to put too much emphasis on meeting immediate needs and be more inclined than trustees to spend down the endowment rather than making tough decisions that may be necessary to ensure the long-term viability of the institution—such as eliminating programs. A long time horizon is of course also critically important in the management of the endowment, which is without question one of the core responsibilities of trustees.

Although it is true that, as Keynes famously said, "in the long run we are all dead," universities are exceptionally durable institutions (with some

---

[3]The original statement may be found in the appendix to the Kelley Committee Report, 161–163, and the current version may be found at http://www.princeton.edu/dof/policies/publ/fac/rules_toc/chaper2/. Consistent with the thrust of the Kelley Committee's recommendations on delegation of authority, the trustees abolished parietals (university-imposed restrictions on dormitory visiting hours for women); other colleges and universities also rethought in loco parentis policies during this period. See David Hoekma, *Campus Rules and Moral Community* (Boston: Rowman and Littlefield, 1994).

in this country predating the Revolutionary War). The resident community should understand that trustees are obligated to protect the institution's long-term interests, and the president should also avoid focusing too narrowly on near-term goals. Henry Bienen, president emeritus of Northwestern University, put it well when he said to me: "University leaders have to be political but they should not be politicians with very short run views of the world."[4] Bienen gave life to his admonition by putting all of the money Northwestern derived from the Lyrica drug patent into endowment—resisting temptations to spend the money on immediate needs.

Drawing careful distinctions as to circumstances in which trustees do and do not expect to exercise active decision-making authority does not mean, of course, that the trustees and the campus community should fail to exchange views on questions of all kinds, and to do so regularly. One lesson I learned was that the president and the administration are well advised to encourage such conversations, provided only that individual trustees (1) not purport to speak for the board; (2) refrain from responding to press inquiries unless authorized to do so; and (3) are careful always to inform the president (or the secretary of the board) of all exchanges of consequence. Trustees should not act behind the president's back and the president cannot be surprised. Efforts are sometimes made to discourage such interactions, if not to prevent them altogether. I think that is a mistake. Such an approach is impractical to start with, since there is no way to prevent casual contacts. Moreover, it implies a fear of the consequences of informal exchanges, and it deprives both the trustees and the campus community of opportunities to learn from each other.

I remember one particularly poignant exchange, when an undergraduate strongly opposed to the Vietnam War argued forcefully with a trustee that the university should take an institutional position against the war. The trustee responded: "It is great that you think as you do and are willing to argue so passionately for what you believe—but it would be a disaster if you prevailed!" Most of the time, of course, informal conversations focus on more mundane subjects, such as courses being studied, favorite professors, campus life, student aid, and a student's job

[4] Personal correspondence, March 11, 2010.

prospects. Such contacts can be extremely valuable in informing trustee consideration of issues, as I know from personal experience as a trustee at Denison, where trustee conversations with faculty and students over meals were customary.

Absolutely central to effective governance is the relationship between the president and the leader of the board of trustees (usually the chair). These two individuals must see themselves as partners in leading a complicated enterprise, and they must enjoy an excellent working relationship based on a high degree of mutual respect. They have complementary roles to play in organizing and managing the work of the board (a major responsibility of the chair) and in providing executive leadership on all fronts (a major responsibility of the president). This relationship is so important that, in my view, it is essential that the president be comfortable with whoever is chosen to chair the board. This particular "partnership" has implications for term lengths. Forming strong partnerships takes time, and it is important to avoid frequent turnover of board chairs.[5]

To trade on personal experiences, I was fortunate at Princeton to have superb leaders of the board all the years I was in the president's office. The three chairs with whom I worked were very different from one another, but all shared an abiding commitment to the university, all understood the difference between the job of the chair and the job of the president, and all provided a skillful blend of guidance and support.[6] They would also, I know, have been forthright in telling me if they thought the time had come for me to step down. One of the three, John C. Kenefick, made a practice of calling me every Sunday morning—once when he was in Hong Kong. We had no secrets, and we learned a great deal from each other. Not every president is as fortunate as I was in this regard, and one

[5] There is much more to be said about how the president and the board chair relate to each other, but to go into more detail here would take us too far afield. Anyone interested in my views on this subject can refer to *The Board Book* (New York: W. W. Norton, 2008), especially chapters 2 and 8.

[6] To be technically correct, I should note that Princeton has no chair of the board itself. The president is the presiding officer. The individuals to whom I refer in this paragraph were chairs of the Executive Committee. But, de facto, the trustee who chairs the Executive Committee functions in much the same way as a board chair in other settings—except that the president presides at board meetings (unless he or she makes recommendations that require board action, when the chair of the Executive Committee presides).

new president who inherited what he described as a "truly dysfunctional board" arranged for an outsider to be brought in to evaluate the board itself—a process, he reports, that led to big changes. In general, boards are notoriously poor at evaluating their own performance.

My strong belief in the notion of "partnership" notwithstanding, I never forgot that I worked for the board—the board does not work for the president. This simple-sounding proposition has major implications, and one of the most important—and often least understood—is that when there is a problem of poor performance or even bad behavior on the part of a board member, it is usually the responsibility of the board chair, not the responsibility of the president, to take appropriate action. This includes the need to ensure (in the absence of strict term limits) that board members do not serve beyond the time when they can be effective contributors. The president should not be the one to ask board members to step down, or to deal with the occasional bully on the board. The board chair can also play a valuable role in orienting new board members and in serving as a resource for those just learning their trade. In addition, the chair can alert the president to problems that the president may not see coming—to a fast train moving down the tracks. Finally, an effective board chair can be invaluable in marshaling external support for the university, including especially alumni support.

There are, however, exceptions to every rule; specifically, there are times when a president must be willing to deal directly with a board malfunction, particularly if it affects the president's ability to work effectively with the board. Let me recount an example from my own experience that may be helpful to others who encounter a similar problem. Putting aside settings in which laws, regulations, or customs require open meetings (found often in the public sector, but rarely in the private sector), both board members and officers should feel entirely free to express themselves without worrying about being quoted (or, worse yet, misquoted) outside the board room or having actions "announced" prematurely or inappropriately. Everyone should expect the usual assumptions about confidentiality to be respected. This is really important. One violation of this cardinal principle of board conduct occurred at Princeton when a trustee leaked to the campus press a board decision to offer an honorary degree to George Shultz, then secretary of the treasury, before Secretary Shultz even knew of the board's intentions. This happened when feelings about the Nixon administration, and the war in Vietnam, were intense, and there was an uproar.

It seemed to me that this truly damaging breach of board rules (which I had not been perceptive enough to anticipate) had to be confronted directly since it was a threat to the way the president and the board interacted. In an executive session, I explained to the trustees, in my role as presiding officer, how strongly I felt about the issue. In my view, the board as a whole had a clear choice to make. On the one hand, it could recommit itself to standard rules of confidentiality with everyone believing that this violation was truly an aberration, that a lesson had been learned, and that there would be no recurrence. Or, if this result could not be achieved, the board had to recognize that the tone and character of its meetings would change dramatically. As all trustees understood, it had been my practice to be entirely open with the board, to try out ideas, to be ready to be corrected, and to hold nothing back—but if there was continuing risk of improper disclosure of "ideas in progress," this way of working with the board would be impossible. Similarly, trustees who had been open with each other, as well as with me, would feel that they had to be more guarded in what they said. An obvious consequence of such a change in the character of meetings would be many more private conversations ahead of meetings, agreements reached out of board meetings as to positions to be taken, and so on. I then asked the trustees to indicate, one by one, whether each was prepared, in effect, to "retake" the oath of office promising to uphold confidentiality. Each responded affirmatively, and we never again had a breach of confidentiality. It was a tense meeting, but it was also a moving example of how a board that experienced a violation of its own rules could recover—and actually become more cohesive as a result.[7]

---

[7] Daniel H. Weiss, president of Lafayette College, commented that a few years before he arrived at Lafayette, there was a breach of confidentiality associated with a discussion of a sensitive matter pertaining to athletics. The issue was not, however, resolved in a satisfactory way at the time, and there was a difficult period in which the board lacked confidence that its deliberations would be private. President Weiss chose to take this issue on directly by reminding trustees that they *must* respect confidentiality if shared governance is to work. He reports that he has distributed highly sensitive information to his board on several occasions and that confidence has

As I have already implied, it is of course easier for boards of private colleges and universities to maintain confidentiality than it is for many of their public cousins, who may be subject to "freedom of information" policies and thus required to meet in open sessions with representatives of the media present. As several commentators with public university experience observed, this can have a chilling effect on discussion. Also, politically appointed trustees may have agendas that are, in their minds, incompatible with confidentiality. For both of these reasons, presidents of public universities face tougher challenges in structuring board discussions than do the leaders of most private institutions.

Much of the time, the board of trustees is essentially invisible to the campus community. Nonetheless—and especially at times when there are contentious issues that have to be resolved at the board level—the broader campus community needs to have confidence in, and respect for, the board. The level of confidence depends not only on how well the board in fact works but also on who is on it.

From time to time there is debate over the wisdom of having current faculty members and students serve on the board. My own view is that this is both unnecessary and unwise. Conflicts of interest would be unavoidable (for instance, when discussing faculty salaries, tuition policies, and so on). More generally, faculty and student board members would find themselves in exceedingly uncomfortable positions if they personally disagreed with a majority of their constituents on an issue before the board. Nor is board membership necessary for trustees to learn what faculty and students are thinking. Faculty and student views can be obtained through many forms of consultation. It is also possible to have on the board individuals who can express general faculty concerns because they serve on the faculty of other institutions. Recent graduates can express student views, and in 1969 the Princeton trustees adopted a recommendation of the Alumni Council providing for the election each year (for a four-year term) of a trustee chosen by juniors, seniors, and the two most recently graduated classes from among candidates nominated by the senior class.

---

returned that the board can work together on these difficult issues. The Lafayette experience is a reminder of how important it is not to let major "process" issues fester.

A number of outstanding individuals have been chosen in this way, and five were subsequently reelected by the board itself.[8]

The composition of boards of public institutions often presents different issues. When there is a political process involved in appointing regents of public institutions, a president can have to deal with board behavior that is complicated, to say the least. Although I was never president of a public university, I learned a great deal about such "complications" through serving as a regent of the Smithsonian Institution. The chancellor of the Smithsonian (the chair of the regents) is normally the chief justice of the Supreme Court, and the presence and active involvement of Chief Justice Burger with the work of the regents at times discouraged frank discussion of issues. Several regents confided that they were reluctant to say anything that might offend the chief justice. There was not, I thought, anything that the chief justice could do to harm me (or Princeton), and so I was able to offer a more "independent" perspective than some of my colleagues who were Washington-based. I know that both fellow regents and the secretary of the Smithsonian (the CEO) appreciated having a colleague who could be entirely candid and did not have to worry about aggravating the chief justice. Similarly, the president of a public university, no less than the president of a private institution, needs at least some board members (regents) who have only the institution's interests at heart and are willing to take on more politically attuned colleagues when necessary.

Consultation and Decision-making on Campus

As important as it is to organize relations between the trustees and the campus community in ways that respect differences in roles, it is every bit as important to have in place good machinery for consultation and decision-making below the level of the board. Having never been known as

---

[8] A number of other important changes in the composition and working of the board were made in the late 1960s, when term limits were established, consultative machinery was developed for selecting new trustees (1969), and retired trustees were no longer invited to attend all board meetings (this change was proposed at the June 1970 board meeting and adopted at the October 1970 meeting).

a patient person (and some of my friends would call that the understatement of many days!), I had a big lesson to learn: that there are benefits to working with what might seem cumbersome processes of on-campus consultation. Time-consuming as they can be, such processes often produce better decisions than quick pronouncements from on high, made sometimes in the absence of needed information and advice. They can generate loyalty and a stronger sense of community. And they can even save time in the long run by avoiding missteps and the need to repair relationships damaged by having failed to consult appropriately ahead of a decision.

There are many ways of structuring consultative machinery, which has to be tailored to the circumstances of particular institutions. The arrangements that I know best are those fashioned by the Kelley Committee at Princeton. Its recommendations led to the creation of a broadly inclusive deliberative body called the Council of the Princeton University Community (CPUC), which is chaired by the president. The council is composed of fifteen faculty members elected from the various divisions of the university, twelve undergraduates, seven graduate students, six administrative officers serving ex officio but with votes, and eleven members from the staff and the alumni body. There are a number of standing committees, including an Executive Committee, a Committee on Rights and Rules, a Judicial Committee, and a Priorities Committee. This machinery has, amazingly, stayed much the same for the last forty years, in spite of dramatic changes in circumstances and the regular turnover of members. To be sure, the relatively centralized character of Princeton, and especially the lack of a panoply of professional schools, makes the establishment and maintenance of such a structure much more practical than it would be at most research universities.

A key to the success of the CPUC at Princeton is the care that has always been taken in the selection of members. There is an elaborate process of nominating candidates that assures that both the CPUC and its committees are broadly representative and do not become the "captives" of any group or groups. The president and other senior administrators are very much part of this selection process, which discourages "we-they" thinking. Widely respected faculty members have been willing to serve on the CPUC and have provided strong leadership.

The Priorities Committee deserves special mention because of the critical role it has played in the annual budgetary process (discussed more substantively in chapter 5). This committee, which is chaired by the provost, has primary responsibility for recommending to the president where dollars should be spent and how resources should be generated. Serving on the committee are other key administrative officers including the dean of the faculty and the vice president for finance, faculty members, students, and a small number of representatives of "other groups."

Recommendations have to be made about faculty salary levels, faculty staffing, tuition and student aid, expenditures on maintenance, and so on. Prior to the establishment of the Priorities Committee, the provost was beset fore and aft by individuals, often self-appointed "representatives" of various interest groups, who felt strongly about one or another aspect of the budget and who insisted on being heard. As the provost at that time, I can speak from personal experience in saying how difficult it was to get people to understand the need for trade-offs. Figuring out where to find the resources to accomplish objective A was never seen as the responsibility of the proponent of A.

Having an orderly process in place, and one that was generally regarded as legitimate, stopped a lot of special pleading. It also imposed a healthy discipline on heads of units seeking resources by requiring them to come to the committee with a well-thought-out case for what they wanted to do. More generally, there is much to be said for being able to lock proponents of competing ideas (raise faculty salaries more aggressively, keep tuition low, change student aid policies, increase funding for the library) in one room, to require them to examine carefully arguments for requests along with supporting evidence, and then to compel the members of the committee to agree on a written report that is distributed widely on and off campus. The broadly representative composition of the committee, and its history of success in getting everyone ultimately to "sign on," has given the committee's reports great credibility and created considerable cohesion around what could otherwise be much more contentious outcomes. Even tough budgetary decisions have generally (not always, but generally) been well accepted.

The last aspect of campus governance that I want to highlight is the need to have a well-functioning faculty structure and well-functioning faculty committees. The concept of shared governance requires that faculty devote time and energy to admissions policies, the shaping of the curriculum, grading standards, campus disciplinary processes, faculty appointments, policies governing sponsored research, and broader questions affecting the welfare of the institution. With only rare exceptions, presidents cannot succeed without strong faculty support, and working closely with faculty colleagues is one way to build—and to earn—support. The fact that Princeton has a single faculty means that there was no need, in that context, to deal with the complications that exist when there are several faculties. The faculty as a whole functions well at Princeton, even as it depends on the hard work of committees.[9]

The role of faculty in the tenure process is so important that I devote a separate section to that topic later in the book. Here I call attention to the special value to me of two other Princeton faculty committees: a well-chosen and broadly representative Faculty Advisory Committee on Policy, whose members serve on the Executive Committee of the CPUC, and a Committee on Committees, which (its off-putting name notwithstanding) was invaluable in organizing and overseeing the process of populating committees with the right mix of people.

It took me some time, probably more than it should have, to realize that all the effort that went into the process of selecting committee members

[9]Richard Lyman, former president of Stanford, reports that "The most important institution created during the years of trouble [at Stanford in the late 1960s and early 1970s] was the Faculty Senate, chosen by all tenure and tenure-track faculty, with a system arranged to prevent the Medical School, with its uniquely high faculty-student ratio, [from dominating] a body which would be doing such things as setting undergraduate degree requirements. The President and Provost, and all the Deans, have ex officio seats without vote" (personal correspondence, February 13, 2010). Lyman goes on to point out that direct access to the president and other officers "guarantees that there will be a link between faculty and administration." At Princeton, the president chairs faculty meetings; the provost and all the deans are present and ready, as at Stanford, to respond to any question that may be raised by a faculty member. I should add that chairing faculty meetings never deterred me from speaking out on any issue; it was always possible to hand the gavel to the provost, if need be. And presiding gave me an opportunity to structure debate, in part through deciding which faculty members to recognize, and in what order. The fact that I knew individual faculty members so well was a great advantage.

and the chairs of committees was well worth it. In the case of the two most important faculty committees (and the most important committee of the CPUC), voting is by single transferable vote—an ingenious way of making sure that no votes are lost, that each voter has an opportunity to express a preference among the "final" candidates for election (after candidates enjoying lesser support have been dropped), and that groups of voters of diverse opinions will succeed in electing representatives in rough proportion to their numbers. This system has the great advantage of ensuring real representation of a variety of views—reducing the risk, as it were, of having any one group become dominant.[10]

Let me also call attention to a more general benefit of having active faculty participation in essentially all aspects of governance. As already noted, the Priorities Committee provided a great opportunity for its members—and especially faculty members who served over some number of years—to learn about budgeting, fiscal realities, and the pain involved in making hard choices. Participation in the work of this committee, and of other committees of both the CPUC and the faculty, almost inadvertently "trained up" a number of faculty to move subsequently into administrative roles at Princeton and elsewhere, as did conferring on departmental chairs active responsibility for recommending salary adjustments (see chapter 7). This almost invisible "development process" helps explain,

[10] The system of the single transferable vote applies when two or more positions on a committee are to be filled simultaneously. In brief, it works this way. Voters are asked to rank all candidates in order of preference. If no candidate has enough first-place votes to be elected (by meeting a "quota" established by formula), the candidate with the fewest first-place votes is eliminated and that candidate's second-place votes are distributed among the remaining candidates; the process continues in this way until the requisite number of candidates meet the quota for election. (See appendix 13 of the Kelley Committee Report for a more elaborate and more rigorous explanation.) If there is only one position to be filled, the system of the alternative vote (described in appendix 12 of the Kelley Committee Report) serves to ensure that the preferences of a majority of voters determine the outcome. Again, if no candidate wins on the basis of first-place votes, the candidate with the fewest first-place votes is eliminated and the second-place votes are distributed; and so on, until someone gets a majority of the votes. In 2010, the Academy of Motion Picture Arts and Sciences adopted this voting procedure to select the best picture. In the United Kingdom, there is serious discussion of these kinds of voting systems in the aftermath of the May 2010 election. Under the present "winner-take-all" system, the Liberal Party won 23 percent of the overall vote but just 9 percent of parliamentary seats. Many winners of seats had quite small percentages of the total vote. See Sarah Lyall, "Unclear Outcome at Polls Adds Urgency to Issue of Electoral Overhaul in Britain," *New York Times*, May 8, 2010, A6.

I think, how such a small university has produced a disproportionate number of presidents, provosts, and deans throughout higher education. Having so many experienced faculty present at meetings of all kinds also raised the level of debate and discouraged "we-they" tendencies—which were remarkably absent during my years at Princeton and are, I believe, absent to this day.

To be sure, Princeton's history of active faculty involvement in university-wide issues has created a culture that would be difficult to replicate in many other settings. Several commentators who served as presidents of other institutions noted that they were not as lucky as I was, and they warned me to inform readers that the Princeton setting was in some degree atypical in this respect. One president who had to work with a very different culture spoke (off the record) of what he called "the Gresham's Law of faculty governance"—if faculty malcontents are allowed to dominate campus governance, they drive away the faculty you want to involve.

The ROTC Debate as an Illustrative Case of Shared Governance

The lengthy, complicated, and at times contentious debate over the Reserve Officers' Training Corps (ROTC) at Princeton is a useful case study of how shared governance and consultation actually worked during a period of considerable stress. The ROTC debate provided a good (tough) test of whether key groups really understood their respective roles, and its history is instructive.

At Princeton as elsewhere, the Vietnam War precipitated a vigorous debate over whether ROTC belonged on campus. In the spring of 1970, the faculty—exercising what were clearly its prerogatives in academic matters—voted to deny ROTC personnel faculty status (since they were not chosen in the regular way) and to withhold academic credit from ROTC courses. These decisions led the Navy and Air Force ROTC programs to leave Princeton. Army ROTC was more willing to continue to operate under these new rules (functioning basically as a noncredit activity that is not a university program). Even so, at the time of the bombing of Cambodia, faculty and student groups voted to recommend phasing out all ROTC programs, albeit in an orderly way, and the trustees at first approved this plan in recognition of the difficulty of continuing to operate an effective program in the face of widespread opposition rooted in strong antiwar sentiments.

There then followed a lengthy process extending over the next two and a half years that involved continued negotiations with the Army, more campus votes (varied in their recommendations), and further trustee review. This process culminated in a decision by the trustees in 1973 to continue the ROTC program under the revised arrangements for course credit (none) and faculty status for military instructors (none) adopted by the faculty. Exercising their right to express their opinion on any issue of consequence, a majority of the faculty voted again to recommend to the trustees that ROTC leave the campus altogether. It was generally understood, however, that the decision regarding the continued presence of ROTC involved issues of external relations and the university's long-term role in society and was, therefore, ultimately a trustee responsibility— unlike the narrower questions of course credit and faculty status, which were clearly in the faculty's domain.

In explaining my own views to the faculty (which favored retaining the Army program under the new faculty stipulations), I emphasized that we should be reluctant to deprive any group of interested students of access to a long-standing opportunity for military service that did not compromise the educational program of the university. Also, I reiterated the need to understand the respective zones of authority of the faculty and the trustees. I thought it was important that the faculty not be surprised if the trustees ended up disagreeing—as they did—with the faculty's overall assessment of ROTC's place on the campus. The trustees' decision to keep the Army ROTC program was well explained and accepted calmly by the campus community, an outcome that might not have been possible in the absence of the statement on delegation and the prior clarification of the respective roles of the faculty and trustees. The by-then understood system of shared governance worked.

Helpful, too, was the fact that by the time of the final trustee decision, the Vietnam War was winding down. Yet another lesson learned is that however convincing arguments of principle are to some people (including high-minded presidents and trustees!), if campus sentiment is over-whelmingly against something, as anti-ROTC sentiment was in 1970 following the invasion of Cambodia, it is not practical to try to maintain the activity. It was only after sentiments had mellowed, in 1972 and 1973, that it was possible to have a more reasoned discussion of the pros and cons of the ROTC issue.[11]

There are three other lessons to be learned from this protracted debate over ROTC.

- First, once an issue of this kind takes hold, it is very difficult—nearly impossible—to prevent it from consuming inordinate amounts of time and attention. The debate has to run its course.

- Second, in dealing with all issues, but especially emotion-laden issues such as this one, it is critically important that the president frame the issues carefully so that participants in the debate are encouraged to address the questions that are really on the table.

- Third, presidents can, within limits, decide how much of their own personal capital they will invest in any debate. In my remarks to the faculty, I stressed that for me ROTC was not a "make or break" issue (as coeducation had been). As I said at the time: "There may be occasions—indeed I am sure there will be—when I feel so strongly about an issue, and its importance to the University, that I will want to do all that I can to press my own views on you and others. But this is not such an occasion. There have been, there are, and there will be great universities without ROTC programs and great universities with ROTC programs."

[11] At the time of this debate, the issue of discrimination against gay students did not arise, as it has more recently at a number of other colleges and universities. The fact that ROTC at Princeton was not a university program was, subsequently, helpful in allowing the university to accept this conflict in values at the same time that it tried to influence the Army to change its policy (which, it now appears, may happen).

THREE

Administering

Much of the rest of this book is about "administering"—which some prefer to call "managing," and which is roughly equivalent to getting important things done reasonably efficiently. I devote separate chapters to topics such as achieving important strategic goals, building the faculty, increasing the "inclusiveness" of the university, handling dissent, and fundraising and alumni relations. In this chapter I talk about "administering" at a more general level, focusing on the recruitment of able colleagues and the establishment of an effective administrative structure.

Building an Effective Administrative Team

I am skeptical that it was ever possible in modern times for a university president to accomplish much on his or her own. Certainly it isn't today. There is just too much to do, too many constituencies to keep in mind, and too many personal relationships that have to be handled sensitively. One of the things I am reasonably good at is identifying and recruiting outstanding people, and whatever success I enjoyed in the president's office was attributable in large part to the quality of my colleagues and to the highly collegial working relationships that we enjoyed. A sure path to mediocrity, if not to failure, is to be afraid of good people. I have always believed in surrounding myself with colleagues who can do all the things that I cannot.

The relationship between the president and the provost (the general deputy to the president in most academic settings) is especially critical. At Princeton I was fortunate to work with a series of outstanding provosts who went on to lead other institutions (including Harvard University, the University of Pennsylvania, and the Sloan Foundation). My last provost, Neil L. Rudenstine, who later served as president of Harvard, was dean of students and then dean of the college at Princeton before becoming provost. Neil and I worked together at Princeton for over twenty years, and I learned so much from this distinguished scholar of English literature who had impeccable judgment and could see around corners that I didn't even know existed. The joke at Princeton was that the university had two provosts and two presidents, since we largely functioned interchangeably. We almost never went to the same meeting, since we got more done by dividing the work. It should also be said that while we had grown up differently, were from different disciplines, brought different perspectives to bear on issues, and had different tendencies (mine, to get it done now—Neil's, to get it done right!), we had exactly the same sense of the university's mission. We never wasted time debating what needed to be accomplished. The importance of having shared values and shared commitments cannot be overstated.

I also learned how valuable it was to have a "nonacademic provost"—a person who could do whatever needed to be done on the administrative side of the house. Of course, much depends on the quality of the person functioning in this role, and I was exceedingly fortunate to have Anthony J. (Tony) Maruca as my longtime vice president for administrative affairs. The skills Tony brought to the table are often undervalued. He was the consummate listener, a kind of ombudsman without the title. Anyone who had a problem could go to Tony, get a good hearing, and be certain that Tony would handle the matter in the appropriate way—whether that meant consulting another administrative officer, taking an action himself, or simply doing nothing. Tony was also willing to take on the unglamorous tasks that had to be done well but that most people preferred to avoid (overseeing security, food services, and so on). He was an all-purpose warrior who had, as he liked to say, "carried his spear" for a long time. He could always be counted on. In my view, every president needs at least one such experienced spear-carrier whom everyone trusts.[1]

By failing to mention them, I certainly do not mean to denigrate the importance of many other wonderful colleagues, on both the academic and administrative sides of the house. Having outstanding deans, investment officers, and administrative assistants matters tremendously. I also learned—through firsthand experience—that institutions should not undervalue contributions made by the truly unusual person who can work across constituencies. My example is Fred Fox '39 (who always insisted that no Princeton name was complete without class numerals), whose title was "Keeper of Princetoniana." Fred's office was directly across from mine in Nassau Hall, and his presence brightened every day. An irrepressible spirit who somehow managed to make the most surly person smile, Fred was a great ambassador to every constituency. He was once prevailed upon to complete—of all things antithetical to his character—a "position description and analysis form." A colleague observed: "The position and the incumbent defy classification, and that is as it should be." Fred's submission was described as "an awesome illustration of the difference that one dedicated individual can make to the life of an institution." Fred listed 161 separate functions involving students, faculty, alumni, and friends. Included on his list was "Soothed Yale Professor whose bulldog was stolen by our undergraduates. Petted his dog."

In recruiting senior colleagues, one major lesson I learned, in the aftermath of a serious mistake, was not to overpersuade. In one case, I believed that I had found the ideal person to fill an important position, and I courted this individual assiduously. As we were about to conclude what I thought were highly promising negotiations, the individual called me and said that, after much thought, he had concluded that the job just wasn't right for him. I refused to accept this conclusion and unleashed all the persuasive skills that I could muster, explaining why the individual was in

---

[1] This is also true in other nonprofits. At the Mellon Foundation, I worked closely with Dennis Sullivan, who was financial vice president but also general "clerk of the works." Dennis is now president and CEO of the Church Pension Group of the Episcopal Church.

fact just right for the job and why he would love it. The candidate accepted the position. Within a year and a half it was evident that his judgment about lack of fit had been correct all along, and that I had been wrong. There was an amicable parting of the ways. The lesson is obvious: individuals being recruited often know more about themselves and what they can and cannot do (and will enjoy doing) than anyone else will ever know, and it is wise to listen carefully to self-assessments. Subsequently, I lived by the adage "no reluctant dragons." I felt so strongly about this lesson that I even had T-shirts made up with "no reluctant dragons" emblazoned on the back. (There are, of course, also candidates who want a job too much, or for the wrong reasons; they too have to be screened out.)

Another (closely related) lesson about choosing people that I learned only imperfectly over time is to listen carefully to the testimony of a wide variety of people who have worked closely with a candidate. It is dangerous to decide too quickly that someone is exactly right for a position— and then fail to heed clear warning signals provided by others. Sometimes I just didn't really "hear" comments that I didn't want to hear because they contradicted what I thought I already knew. It can be especially valuable to take testimony from people who have worked for a candidate in a subordinate role. Some people are good at relating "up" but not so good at relating "down."

I also learned not to focus too much on fixing one's last mistake. When seeking to replace someone who had displayed an obvious deficiency, it is tempting to concentrate on finding a successor without that particular problem. But that approach can lead to appointing someone who lacks other needed skills. I learned this lesson in domains as different as football (coaches need to be able both to inspire and to call the right plays inside the twenty-yard line) and libraries (librarians need to be able both to take advantage of new technologies and to manage staff in an old-fashioned, loving way). There is no escaping the need to look at the whole set of talents required and then to make a determined effort to find someone who has them all. Those of us who grew up as teachers sometimes mistakenly think (as I have done) that we can teach more than we can. The colleague I mentioned earlier, Tony Maruca, wisely admonished me: "People come in packages; you either buy the package or you don't, but do not believe that you can improve the package very much." After some point in life, people are more or less who they are, warts and all. In deciding what choices to make in recruiting outside talent, one wise university president said that he often compromised on experience, but never on talent, because he believed that "people rarely get smarter but they do gain experience over time."[2] True, and one of the most gratifying experiences a president can have is to see colleagues get better as they learn at least some things from each other and from their own successes (and missteps).

Inevitably, some mistakes will be made, no matter how well considered the search process. In fact, the absence of *any* mistakes would imply to me that there is too little risk-taking. But it is important to think carefully about when it is, and when it is not, wise to take a risk. It can be especially dangerous, for example, to take a risk when appointing someone like an athletic director who will be in a position to marshal external support for policies with which the president may not agree. (This was not, let me emphasize, a problem with any of the athletic directors I appointed, but it certainly has been a problem in some settings.) The general point is that the president needs to be confident that the AD shares his or her values and will represent the college or university well, both internally and externally. It can be awkward in the extreme to have an AD say something like "the university is committed to achieving excellence across the board" and then measure "excellence" on an overly simple scale demarcated primarily by won-lost records.[3] The president has to be confident that the AD will not work around the university's leadership, garnering support from athletic advocates for problematic policies. The press is full of stories

---

[2] I am reminded that Princeton's longtime basketball coach, Pete Carril, used to say that while he could teach his players many things, he could not teach them to jump higher or run faster. Carril was also fond of quoting his father in explaining how, on occasion, one of his teams would beat a team that had more raw talent—as happened in one National Invitational Tournament final. When a reporter asked Carril how his undersized team could possibly have won, he responded that he had learned many things from his father, an immigrant from Spain who had worked in the steel mills all his life. "My father taught me," Carril said, "that in this life the strong take from the weak and the smart take from the strong."

[3] For an extended discussion of the problems with the "excellence across the board" theme, see James L. Shulman and William G. Bowen, *The Game of Life: College Sports and Educational Values* (Princeton: Princeton University Press, 2001), especially 300–301.

illustrating how easy it is for a university to be trapped in this kind of situation. Moreover, if the wrong person is appointed as AD, and succeeds in building up a personal constituency that includes trustees as well as influential alumni, it can be very difficult to make a change.

Still, as I have said, with the best will in the world, it is unrealistic to expect to make the right appointment every time. Inevitably it will turn out that, as an experienced colleague once put it, "all of our ducks are not swans." As all of us know, people who are excellent in one setting ("swans" in one pond) may be less effective when asked to do something else ("ducks" in another pond). Some absolutely outstanding faculty members are not good at certain kinds of administrative tasks. For example, one of my closest friends at Princeton, a highly regarded academic with an international reputation, was neither happy nor terribly successful during a brief stint as provost. He found relations with the student press particularly vexing, and I will never forget his response to a reporter for the *Daily Princetonian* who was convinced that one mistake had occurred because the provost was managing a vast conspiracy of some kind. Exasperated, he said: "Can't you accept the simple explanation of incompetence?" In another case, I failed to recognize that a faculty member with a sterling reputation at another very good—but very different—university would not function well at Princeton.

When I was asked what lessons I had learned in the course of appointing countless numbers of people, I said: "I have learned two things: to acknowledge my mistakes sooner and to fix problems faster." Once it is evident that someone is just not working out, it rarely, if ever, pays to just hope that things will improve, that the sun will shine tomorrow. A trustee commentator with extensive business experience told me that in the venture capital world in which he lives, there is this saying: "I never fired anyone too soon." A related lesson I learned is that it is sometimes (though certainly not always) easier than one might have supposed to deal with unwelcome personnel problems. The person having difficulties may well recognize that there is a problem and be relieved when the problem is identified and addressed directly. In such situations, I learned to say something like: "Let's not waste time debating what went wrong or how we got where we are—no finger-pointing. Rather, let's simply agree that, for whatever reasons, things are just not working and that we need, together, to find a graceful way out."

There can also be instances of wrong behavior that require even more forceful action. Wesleyan University is suing its former chief investment officer for allegedly stealing proprietary information and enriching himself by not only using information obtained through his work at Wesleyan for his own purposes but devoting excessive amounts of time to personal investment activities that he concealed from Wesleyan's leadership.[4] Blatant abuses of one's position are rare (thank heavens!), but when they occur it is important to deal with them directly, to hold individuals accountable for their conduct, and not to cover up the need for vigorous corrective action—in university governance no less than in business or government.

Structuring Interactions

In addition to making as many good appointments as possible—and fixing expeditiously whatever mistakes are made along the way—it is important to structure interactions among the administrative team in ways that promote fruitful exchanges of ideas but are not overly bureaucratic or a waste of time. Some number of regularly scheduled meetings of key people are desirable (the "cabinet" concept), but often there are too many of these meetings. It was helpful, I found, simply to cancel meetings when it seemed unlikely that they would be productive. This practice not only saved time; it also sent a message that we were not in the business of "meeting just to be meeting." Needless to say, none of this is to deny the value of easy informal discussions. As one of my great teachers, Jacob Viner, used to say: "There is no limit to the amount of nonsense one can think, if he thinks too long alone."

Let me add another comment about allocation of time that is meant to reinforce what I have just said about being parsimonious in scheduling

---

[4]For an extended discussion of what allegedly happened, see Doug Lederman, "Tangled Web at Wesleyan," *Inside Higher Ed*, January 6, 2010, http://www.insidehighered.com/news/2010/01/06/wesleyan.

regular meetings: presidents should not feel guilty if they end up spending relatively small amounts of time with one or another senior colleague. In some situations, the president may not spend a great deal of time with Dean X because the president does not think that the time spent will be particularly productive. But the reason for limited contact may also be that all is going well in the person's domain and there is just no need for presidential intervention. I tried to explain to sensitive deans that my absence from their doorway was almost always a good sign, not a bad one. It meant that I was pleased with their work and confident that they would make the right judgments. My practice was to spend serious time in the areas, and with the people, where there were consequential problems, where I thought I was really needed and perhaps could help. But it is of course important to be easily accessible to colleagues who want to see the president, as well as to faculty, staff, and other members of the university community.

As several colleagues at other universities have observed, it is important not to draw too sharp a line between academic and administrative functions. It is wise, I think, to remind people that everyone in a college or university works to support the academic mission. It is decidedly unhelpful to give staff members the feeling that they are part of a lower caste. The flipside of this coin is that high-ranking administrative officers (and those who work for them) should not be imperious in dealing with faculty—they should not create resentments.

In working with senior colleagues, it is important to encourage them to take good care of themselves. There are too many examples of situations in which individuals overwork and do not find time for "refreshment." Presidents should set a suitable example (as I say directly in chapter 10), but some of us are not good at that. Having been certified many times as an incorrigible workaholic, I used to try to convince colleagues to do what I said, not what I did. At the least, the president can recognize that different individuals have different priorities and can be at different stages in their lives in terms of family and other responsibilities. One of my most valued colleagues at the Mellon Foundation spent considerable time managing the affairs of a church, and I did my best to emphasize that this was fine. Schedules that work for one person may not work for another. It is foolish to think in terms of a single, unvarying conception of the workweek.

The difficult experience Duke had in managing a bitter controversy over its lacrosse program amid allegations about the behavior of some players illustrates the fundamental importance of clear (and prompt, as well as accurate) communication up and down the line. Duke's president, Richard Brodhead, was handicapped severely by delays in giving him full reports as to what was alleged to have happened. The Duke lacrosse story is also a striking example of how poorly performing public officials, over whom the university has no control, can cause enormous problems. The Durham district attorney resigned, and was eventually disbarred, because of the unpardonable mistakes he made in addressing what turned out to be unfounded allegations of sexual misconduct—but by then much damage had been done.[5]

Compensation—for Administrators and for the President

In compensating administrative colleagues at all levels it is necessary to be competitive and recognize market realities. It follows that administrators in areas such as investment management and development (never mind football and basketball coaches in big-time programs!), as well as those responsible for professional schools such as law, business, and medicine, will almost always command more money than colleagues in, say, student affairs. But these market-driven differences in pay levels should be tempered to the extent this can be done without losing people essential to the success of the institution. Good colleagueship is vital, and keeping salary differences under some control is one way of encouraging people to feel that everyone works for the same institution.

Thinking about thresholds was helpful to me in dealing with salary issues. That is, individuals need to earn enough to be tolerably comfortable and to feel that they can educate their children. But once a reasonable

[5] I was asked by President Brodhead to be part of an investigation of the university's handling of this matter, and the public report issued by Julius L. Chambers and me can be found at http://www.dukenews.duke.edu/mmedia/pdf/Bowen-ChambersReportFinal05-04-06.pdf. Later parts of the story, including the resignation and disbarment of the prosecutor, can be found at http://www.nytimes.com/2007/04/12/us/12duke.html, http://www.nytimes.com/2007/06/16/us/16duke.html, and http://www.nytimes.com/2007/06/17/us/17duke.html.

threshold has been reached, care should be taken not to be too aggressive in pushing up salaries. John C. Bogle, the founder of Vanguard, tells a wonderful story about a party given by a billionaire on Shelter Island. Several writers were among the guests, and the late Kurt Vonnegut informed his friend, the author Joseph Heller, that their host, a hedge fund manager, had made more money in a single day than Heller had earned from his wildly popular novel *Catch 22* over its whole history. Heller is said to have responded: "Yes, but I have something he will never have. . . . *Enough*."[6] In a similar vein, I am reminded that when AT&T tried to use a huge salary incentive to persuade Charles Exley, then president and CEO of NCR, to facilitate a takeover of NCR by AT&T, Exley said, in effect, "I have a boat; what would I do with two boats?"

As legions of horror stories remind us, presidents need to be especially careful that their own salary is kept at a reasonable level. President Lawrence Bacow of Tufts has explained eloquently why he insisted that his board pay him less than it wanted to pay him. He understood that allowing his own salary to get too much higher than the salaries of his colleagues (key faculty members as well as administrators) would have sent the wrong signal to those at Tufts on whom he depended. But not everyone understands either this central point or the damage that can be done externally if a sense of greed is communicated. Much as I respect the hard work and sacrifices of college and university presidents, I wonder if the general level of salaries has not become higher than it should be, given the special place of these not-for-profit institutions in our society. Trustees' increased use of compensation consultants in reviewing presidential salaries should help produce defensible outcomes, but I confess to wondering if sometimes such consultants use comparisons that ratchet up salaries more than is necessary.

Then, there always seem to be "outlier" cases that embarrass all of us. In December 2009, the *New York Times* reported that the attorney general of New Jersey had filed suit against the Stevens Institute of Technology in Hoboken and its president, Harold J. Raveché, accusing him of plundering

---

[6]From a speech given by John C. Bogle at Georgetown University commencement, May 18, 2007. Bogle repeats the story in a book titled, appropriately, *Enough: True Measures of Money, Business and Life* (Hoboken: John Wiley and Sons, 2009).

the endowment and receiving $1.8 million in illegal low-interest loans for vacation homes, with half of the loans later forgiven. Dr. Raveché's salary was tripled over a decade, and at $1.1 million was deemed "excessive" by two independent compensation consultants—whose conclusions were never reported to the full board. There are many morals to be drawn from this sad saga. The president of an institution should (1) resist any temptation to pack the board with loyalists who will seek to please the president by pushing up his compensation; (2) insist that his own compensation is kept under control; and (3) resist lavish renovation of the presidential residence and avoid altogether perks like expensive vacation houses that are sure to enrage the faculty, among others. It is baffling how presidents can fail to see the consequences of what is bound to be perceived as outrageous, self-serving behavior.[7]

Fortunately, many presidents have been much wiser and have understood full well the symbolic importance of presidential salaries. The fiscal crisis that has afflicted all of higher education in 2009–2010, and especially the public sector, has led a number of presidents to volunteer for pay freezes and cuts in their salaries. A growing number of presidents have also given money back to their campuses, often for specific programs, sometimes privately and sometimes publicly. In today's world, colleges and universities have to file publicly available tax forms (990s) that include detailed information on compensation and perquisites, including payments made after individuals retire; knowledge that there will be public disclosure is simply one more incentive to do the right thing.

---

[7] See Sam Dillon, "New Jersey College Is Beset by Accusations," *New York Times,* December 22, 2009, 1ff. As the story makes clear, the Stevens Institute of Technology is by no means the only institution that has suffered from such practices. Subsequently, a settlement was reached that includes extensive governance changes, the departure of Raveché as president in July 2010, and a requirement that Raveché repay approximately $750,000 on outstanding mortgages. Raveché will, however, receive his current (very high) salary for a year after he leaves office and be retained as a consultant through June 2014. See Sam Dillon, "New Jersey Has Settled with a College It Sued," *New York Times,* January 16, 2010, A18.

FOUR

The University in Society:
"At a Slight Angle to the Universe"

Basic Principles

In all that it does, a university (and certainly its president) needs to have a clear understanding of the special place that the university occupies in society. This chapter is about the twin norms of openness to all points of view and institutional restraint that are at once seemingly antithetical to each other and yet actually mutually dependent.[1] The university stands, in words E. M. Forster once applied to the Greek poet Cavafy, "at a slight angle to the universe."[2] It is a most unusual institution. In its openness to ideas of all kinds and in its nonpartisan, independent character, it is fundamentally different from government agencies, churches, business organizations, labor organizations, political parties, philanthropies, and social clubs. Its purpose is not to indoctrinate but to educate—and in that process to encourage "a hundred flowers to bloom." It has important

[1] Anyone interested in a fuller exposition of my views on this subject can consult my talk at opening exercises at Princeton in September 1985, reprinted in *Ever the Teacher* (Princeton: Princeton University Press, 1988), 5–12.

[2] Forster famously described Cavafy as "a Greek gentleman in a straw hat, standing absolutely motionless at a slight angle to the universe." "The Poetry of C. F. Cavafy," in *Pharos and Pharillon* (New York: Alfred A. Knopf, 1961), 91–92.

responsibilities to society but it discharges them in important degree by means that are often as likely to provoke as to reassure.

Today, almost all leading colleges and universities in this country enjoy a degree of autonomy, and especially freedom from the application of political as well as religious tests, that is distinctive when viewed historically or compared with universities in many other parts of the world. The historian Lawrence Stone reminded us that "the old ideal" of indoctrination held sway for a very long time, and for very good reasons. "After all," Stone wrote, "whenever society is precarious—and it usually is—there is inevitably a demand that dissidents and heretics be suppressed." "The new ideal," to create open and adaptable minds ready to question and challenge established facts and conventional wisdom, did not really take hold in this country until the early part of the nineteenth century. "I want to stress," Stone said, "how novel this [the new ideal] was, and how rare and fragile. . . . For most of recorded history, those in authority have thought it wiser to create closed minds than open minds, to educate students to conform to traditional values and to follow the accepted wisdom."[3] It is worth remembering that at the time of World War I, Presidents John Grier Hibben of Princeton and Nicholas Murray Butler of Columbia committed their universities to a "war policy" and did all that they could to repress dissent.[4] Nor can we assume that these arguments are over. The McCarthy era of loyalty oaths and investigations of faculty beliefs occurred in the

[3] See Lawrence Stone, "Princeton's Roots: An Amalgam of Models," *Princeton Alumni Weekly*, September 12, 1977; reprinted in *The Best of PAW* (Princeton: Princeton Alumni Weekly, 2000), 5. In a similar vein, Bernard Lewis, the distinguished scholar of the Middle East, observes in his book *The Jews of Islam* (Princeton: Princeton University Press, 1984), "Tolerance is a new virtue, intolerance a new crime. . . . Until comparatively modern times, Christian Europe neither prized nor practiced tolerance itself, and was not greatly offended by its absence in others. The charge that was always brought against Islam was not that its doctrines were imposed by force—something seen as normal and natural—but that its doctrines were false" (3–4).

[4] See Cole, *The Great American University*, 45–49, for many such examples. A Princeton alumnus, Henry Strater '19, a pacifist as an undergraduate, joined with several other students to bring the most famous antiwar personality of the time, William Jennings Bryan, to speak at Princeton. Mr. Strater offered this recollection of what happened next: "The president of Princeton called me into his office when he found out about Bryan. President Hibben said that he couldn't allow Bryan to speak on campus because he had already committed Princeton to a war policy. Eventually we were able to have Bryan speak at a little church that adjoined the campus, and he spoke to a full house" (*Princeton Alumni Weekly*, June 19, 1985, 9–11). In Russia and China, the state continues to take a definite interest in what academics say and do, and of course in coun-

1950s, and the activities of some radical student groups in the late 1960s remind us that threats to genuine openness can come from the Left as well as from the Right.[5]

Our insistence today on openness and independence is rooted in a distinct educational philosophy that embraces critical thinking and active debate as the best ways of pursuing truth, correcting old errors, and developing new ideas. This philosophy stems not just from an abstract sense that it is intrinsically the right way to educate people in a democracy, but also from a powerful utilitarian argument. A country that wants to be on the research frontier, and to attract the best faculty and the best graduate and undergraduate students from all over the world, will not succeed unless faculty and students alike know that they are free to explore ideas of every kind. Widespread acceptance of this pragmatic argument among government leaders, business executives, and others interested in economic progress has had a great deal to do with bringing trustees and legislators to accept the need for unfettered freedom to teach and study as one thinks best. It will be interesting to see if China can develop the outstanding system of higher education to which it is committed while continuing to limit freedom of thought and expression—a policy that will, I think, make it especially hard to achieve excellence in the social sciences and humanities.

Our philosophy of education, with its emphasis on openness to ideas of every kind, creates a strong presumption against the university as an institution taking positions on external issues of a political, social, or economic character that do not relate directly to its educational mission. As Richard Hofstadter said beautifully at the Columbia commencement of 1968 (in the immediate aftermath of great turmoil):

> While I hope I am speaking in the interest of my university, it
> would be wrong to suggest that I am precisely speaking for it.
> It is in fact of the very essence of the conception of the modern

tries such as Iran there is nothing resembling academic freedom. Similarly, Chile and Greece have suffered from political assaults on universities within the last few decades.

[5] Readers unfamiliar with the McCarthy period and its effects on universities may want to consult Ellen Schrecker, *No Ivory Tower: McCarthyism and the Universities* (New York: Oxford University Press, 1986).

university that . . . no one is authorized to speak for it. . . . It does not have corporate views of public questions. . . . This fact of our all speaking separately is in itself a thing of great consequence, because in this age of rather overwhelming organizations and collectivities, the university is singular in being a collectivity that serves as a citadel of intellectual idealism.[6]

The university—and its president—can and should speak out on matters central to its own functioning as an educational institution, such as free speech (loyalty oaths) and admissions policies (affirmative action), but these have a directly relevant educational content that differentiates them from broad political and social issues.

One of the hardest things for many people to understand is the powerful complementarity between the rights of *individual* faculty members and students to speak out strongly on issues of all kinds and the need for *institutional restraint* in addressing broad political and social issues. The university should be the home of the critic, not the critic itself. If the university takes an institutional position when it doesn't have to, it makes it harder for faculty and students who have other views to feel free to speak out—especially if they are nontenured faculty members or graduate students who may worry about antagonizing senior members of their departments. Even if the university succeeds in resisting pressures to take an institutional or "corporate" position on an issue, such as the bombing of Cambodia at the time of the Vietnam War, campus sentiment itself can make it uncomfortable for those in the minority (in this case, those who favored the escalation of the war) to declare themselves. I spent more time than I care to recall defending the rights of this pro-war minority, and it would have been much harder for me to do so if the university had been encumbered with an antiwar institutional position. It is important to heed the admonition of H. H. Wilson, a Princeton professor known for his assaults on the establishment, that we should do nothing that might "drive disagreement under cover."

[6]Richard Hofstadter, "Columbia University Commencement Address for the 214th Academic Year," in *American Higher Education Transformed 1940–2005: Documenting the National Discourse*, edited by Wilson Smith and Thomas Bender (Baltimore: Johns Hopkins University Press, 2008), 384.

Institutional restraint also reduces the risk that the university will need-lessly antagonize groups in society on which it is dependent for political as well as financial support. As Richard Lyman put it in 1974, in remarks to an entering class at Stanford:

> Why on earth should we expect that a society full of powerful and wealthy interest groups will be willing to watch without doing anything while the diversity and openness of universities are abandoned in favor of institutional commitment and the pro-duction of political propaganda?

He then added:

> Efforts would be made to enlist universities on the side of political interests very different from the political interests that are most active and prominent on the campus today. There is nothing in the law of nature that says a politicized university must always be politicized in favor of peace, freedom and equality.[7]

It is, I think, quite remarkable how willing public bodies in this country, and alumni, have been to tolerate the criticism and dissension that emerge from campus communities. I believe that this willingness to accept the vigorous exercise of academic freedom is dependent on evidence of in-stitutional restraint on the part of universities and their presidents. Since colleges and universities are widely perceived as overwhelmingly liberal, it has also helped that staunch conservatives such as George Stigler have done their best to explain why university faculty and students are inher-ently "oppositionist."[8]

---

[7] Lyman, *Stanford in Turmoil*, 176.

[8] Stigler wrote: "The university is by design and effect the institution in society which creates discontent with the existing moral, social, and political institutions and proposes new institutions to replace them. . . . Invited to be learned in the institutions of other times and places, incited to new understandings of the social and physical world, the university faculty is inherently a disruptive force." "The University in Political and Social Movements," George Stigler Papers, Box 22, File 67:04, University of Chicago Archives. See also the incisive Chicago report on this topic, "Kalven Committee: Report on the University's Role in Political and Social Action," November 11, 1967, http://www-news.uchicago.edu/releases/07/pdf/kalverpt.pdf. Thus, it is not surprising that in Iran today, it is campus communities that are the most critical of the government. When

At times of intense political controversy such as the Vietnam War, it is always tempting for campus groups to try to use the nearest "instrument" (the university) as a weapon to press their own positions on the government or on others. A lesson many of us learned during long debates over whether the university as an institution should "speak out" is that the president, in particular, has to try hard to help the campus community understand the basic principles involved and the long-term value of institutional restraint.

Great patience is required, since the ever-changing composition of the student population, in particular, means that the same points have to be made over and over. I spent more time on this "educational" task than on almost any other during the most trying days. But it is very important, I believe, that presidents do what they can to help members of the campus community, especially newer members, think through complex institutional issues that they have never really had to confront before. In trying to explain the stakes, it is helpful to point out that other actors in society may have difficulty respecting the university as a nonpartisan educational institution genuinely open to all points of view if the university itself is espousing a particular point of view. Jonathan Cole has argued that during the twentieth century a kind of "compact" grew up between society and academia, whereby academia produced the research that society badly needed and society allowed faculty to choose their own colleagues and to speak out, as individuals, on issues of all kinds.[9]

There are differences, I believe, between the freedoms that faculty and students should feel free to exercise and the more limited freedom of presidents and deans to speak out. In the widely publicized case of Lawrence Summers at Harvard, and the questions he raised about women's ability to do math and science, some argued that Summers was a professor as well as president (true), and that he therefore had the same right as other faculty to exercise his "academic freedom" by saying whatever he wanted to say on controversial issues of every kind (wrong). This is a foolish line of ar-

---

I visited China in the immediate aftermath of the Cultural Revolution, party leaders were very concerned about how they could "get the faculty to think right."

[9] See Cole, *The Great American University*, 53.

gument because it is impossible for a president, who often has to speak for the university, to distinguish his views as a faculty member from his views as president. Outsiders, especially, will never understand the distinction.[10] Similarly, I do not think that deans should sign petitions on subjects such as divestment that could be thought to color their views of the qualifications for advancement of faculty who in some measure report to them. When faculty accept senior administrative positions (which are inevitably somewhat "corporate" in nature), they should understand that they are now more constrained in what they can say on political and social issues than they were before. The same argument can be made in the case of the leader of the board of trustees.

I recognize that this argument in favor of both openness to ideas of every kind and institutional restraint is more complicated in the case of institutions with strong religious commitments than it is in secular settings. Notre Dame's invitation to President Obama to receive an honorary degree and give the commencement address in 2009 is an interesting case in point. Some Catholics argued that Obama's pro-choice position made him ineligible to receive an honorary degree from Notre Dame. But Notre Dame did not agree that welcoming President Obama, and honoring him in this way, contradicted the anti-abortion position of the church. In his speech, Obama argued in favor of a reasoned, respectful discourse on this highly sensitive issue. He then cited Father Hesburgh's description of Notre Dame as both a lighthouse and a crossroads: "a lighthouse that stands apart, shining with the wisdom of the Catholic tradition, while the crossroads is where differences of culture and religion and conviction can co-exist with friendship, civility, hospitality, and especially love." This eloquent statement recognizes both the claims of religious conviction and the value, in every university setting, of candid exchanges on even the most sensitive issues. The lighthouse and the crossroads can and should coexist.[11]

[10] The best discussion of the subtleties of this important issue is contained in a piece by Richard Posner, federal judge on the U.S. Court of Appeals for the Seventh Circuit: "Larry Summers and Women Scientists—Posner," http://www.becker-posner-blog.com/archives/2005/01/.

[11] See *Chicago Tribune*, May 17, 2009, for a transcript of President Obama's Notre Dame speech.

The Proposed Boycott of J. P. Stevens

The most hotly debated challenges to the principles of openness and institutional restraint usually occur in the context of invitations to controversial individuals to speak on campus, and later in this chapter I examine lessons learned from five specific events of this kind—with the invitation to Alger Hiss to speak at Princeton in the 1950s and the invitation to Iranian president Ahmadinejad to speak at Columbia in 2007 serving as "bookends." First, however, I want to discuss an entirely different situation in which Princeton was urged (in 1977–1978) to join in a national boycott of the products of the textile manufacturer J. P. Stevens because some members of the campus community objected to the company's labor practices.

This proposal seemed wrongheaded to me precisely because it asked the university and its president to take a stand on an external issue that was primarily social and political, not educational. Individual students and faculty members were, of course, entirely free to do their best to influence the J. P. Stevens Company to change its policies or to work for changes in the applicable law if that was what seemed wise to them. But what can be right and proper for individuals may be wrong and damaging for an educational institution and its president.[12]

In the course of the ensuing debate, my colleagues and I had one good idea: let individual students and faculty members decide for themselves how they thought this issue should be addressed by giving them a choice of towels in the gym. But not a dichotomous choice. We created three piles: (1) towels manufactured by J. P. Stevens that could be chosen by individuals who favored the company's practices; (2) towels manufactured by other companies with different labor practices that could be chosen by in-

[12] W. Taylor Reveley III, president of William & Mary, provided an excellent illustration of the key distinction between issues central to the functioning of the university and issues of other kinds when, in March 2010, he spoke out strongly on the right of public colleges and universities in Virginia to oppose discrimination on the basis of sexual orientation. See "No Discrimination at W&M," http://www.wm.edu/news/pressreleases/2010/no-discrimination-at-wm.php. At the same time, Reveley continued to decline to pronounce on societal and political issues that he did not consider central to the functioning of the university even if, in President Reveley's words, "others regard [them] as profoundly important."

dividuals who favored the boycott; and (3) a random pile that included an unidentified mix of towels, some from J. P. Stevens and some from other purveyors. The third set of towels could be chosen by individuals who, for whatever reason, chose not to participate in this debate. The "random" pile of towels was by far the most popular—which perhaps indicated that many people just weren't that interested in the issue.

There is a big lesson to be learned from this controversy. Obvious as it may seem to some (it was not at all obvious to many faculty members and students), neither individuals nor educational institutions should be compelled to take a position on every issue that others regard as highly consequential. To abstain is both a legitimate and appropriate action for a college or university when the issue is not central to the institution's educational mission. Universities need to retain control over their own agendas and to decide for themselves when it is, and when it is not, appropriate to take a position; looked at in this way, debates over affirmative action and discrimination based on sexual orientation seem to me entirely different from debates over labor practices in the textile industry. I remember well the relief expressed by one conscientious faculty member when he understood that he did not have to be either for or against the J. P. Stevens boycott. "For or against" was not the way to phrase the issue. The subsequent discussion within the CPUC (which culminated in a vote of 24–14 against the proposed boycott) also allowed many individuals who started out with polarized positions to conclude, eventually, that individual choice was what made sense. Structured debate can be edifying, especially if background materials are provided in advance.[13]

The same line of argument persuades me that presidents should reserve the right to "pass" on issues outside their own area of expertise and separate from core questions of educational policy. Even within the educational domain, it is perfectly reasonable for a president to decline to take a firm position on a complicated question until there has been time to study it and obtain the advice of others. When one embattled president came to see me at the Mellon Foundation, I counseled him to pick and choose in

---

[13] The Executive Committee of the CPUC directed that a paper I wrote on this issue (which is reprinted in *Ever the Teacher*, 20–28), along with papers by proponents of the boycott, be distributed to all members of the CPUC.

deciding which areas of controversy to enter. He was fighting too many wars on too many fronts. There is no reason to expect a president to be knowledgeable about, or even interested in, every question. Moreover, doing battle on every imaginable issue can create adversarial relationships that diminish the president's ability to work with colleagues of many persuasions.

Divestment and South Africa

Yet another challenge to the principle of institutional restraint arose repeatedly in the context of demands that the university divest holdings of stocks and other financial instruments of companies that did any part of their business in South Africa. Nearly all of us who participated in this decades-long debate (running from the late 1960s through the 1980s) shared a common perspective: there was widespread agreement that the apartheid policy of the then-government of South Africa was abhorrent and contradicted basic values of any civilized community, including any university community. What was at issue, however, was not how we felt about apartheid, and not what, as *individuals,* we should do about apartheid (even though there were obviously differences of opinion). What was at issue was what the university *as an institution* should do.

In their lengthy consideration of this issue of investment policy, the trustees consistently concluded that divestiture was not the right approach to what they agreed was a morally gripping problem. Their reasons for opposing divestiture included doubts about its effectiveness in changing either company policies or policies of the South African government. Some thought that the presence of American companies would, on balance, improve rather than retard prospects for ending racism in South Africa. There were other objections as well, including reservations about arguments related to "moral purity" and concerns about where to draw lines: How should index funds be treated? What about assets invested in Teachers Insurance and Annuity Association–College Retirement Equities Fund (TIAA-CREF) that provided pensions to faculty and staff? There were also worries about setting precedents. What should be done in the case of other oppressive regimes?

Most fundamental of all were concerns about fiduciary responsibilities and the long-term effects of divestiture on the university's own well-being (since ruling out broad classes of securities as investment options could have serious adverse effects on the returns needed to support university programs). The trustees were also reluctant to be seen as penalizing companies for doing even a small part of their business in South Africa when the university had made such determined efforts to convince potential donors, corporations as well as individuals, to judge the university "overall," not on the basis of one criterion or one set of actions. Finally, many trustees doubted that it was appropriate for the university to seek to have "a political effect" in confronting an external issue not related directly to its own educational program. Selling shares of stock seemed like both an indirect and inappropriate way to put pressure on governments and businesses, here and abroad. Individuals could and should, many agreed, do their best to persuade Congress to be more active in opposing apartheid; but political actions by individuals are very different from "corporate" actions of a political kind by educational institutions.

The university agreed that it should be a responsible voter of proxies (since abstentions were counted as votes for management), and it agreed to eschew very limited kinds of investments that were seen to support apartheid directly. It also supported a number of educational initiatives that were consistent with its mission—and this is surely a positive role that universities should play in seeking to be helpful in politically troubled situations, and in poor countries that are badly in need of research expertise as well as enhanced teaching capacity. But the trustees remained convinced that divestment was not an approach they should favor.

As president, I was the primary spokesman for university policy in this area. I appeared at open forums and answered questions (on one occasion for more than three hours).[14] Perhaps the major lesson I learned was that

---

[14]Some of these sessions were tense, and one of my colleagues observed that it just seemed necessary to give students an opportunity every now and then to yell at the president. But in the main, I was treated in a very civil fashion, and some of the protestors are firm friends today.

on contentious issues of all kinds, and especially on sensitive issues such as apartheid, there is no substitute for being willing to listen and then for articulating the reasons for the university's position as clearly as possible. Protests, picketing, and chants around Nassau Hall continued, and at one point a group of protestors, meeting with me in my office, asked directly: "What will it take to get you to change your position on this issue? Larger demonstrations?" My answer was very simple: "No, better reasons." Fortunately, many faculty, as well as some students, understood the arguments the trustees were making and expressed agreement with them. Another lesson, then, is the importance of involving many thoughtful members of the university community in such debates so that it is not just the president and the trustees against the protestors.[15]

This is another area in which broad issues of approach and of principle keep resurfacing. In recent years there have been other divestment petitions, for example, by those seeking support for Palestinian causes who have asked college and university trustees to divest from companies that do business in Israel. Although there are of course differences in circumstances, I remain skeptical about the wisdom of the divestment approach.

Freedom to Speak—and to Hear

I now return to perhaps the most central set of challenges to "the new ideal" of an educational institution open to all points of view: main-

---

[15]Of all the talks I gave (and papers I wrote), my discussion of divestiture attracted more interest from other colleges and universities than the talks I gave on any other subject except affirmative action. I have asked the Princeton University Press to put on its Web site the full text of my main paper on divestiture. There were, of course, many detailed points about the South Africa debate that I have not covered here, for reasons of space (whether banks should be treated differently from industrial companies, how proxies should be voted, and so on). I should also note one irony. When I left the president's office at Princeton for the president's office at the Mellon Foundation, I was active in supporting the efforts of anti-apartheid leaders in the "open" South African universities, including Stuart Saunders, then vice-chancellor of the University of Cape Town (author of *Vice-Chancellor on a Tightrope: A Personal Account of Climactic Years in South Africa* [Cape Town: David Philip Publishers, 2000]). Presidents of foundations are in quite different positions than presidents of universities. And the long debates over apartheid at Princeton had prepared me well to play a different role once I was at the Mellon Foundation.

taining the cardinal principle that members of the university community can invite speakers of their choice to campus, that invited speakers have the right to speak without serious disruption, and that campus members have the right to hear such speakers if they choose to do so as well as the right to express opposition—albeit in appropriate ways. This principle has been challenged many times, and there is no reason to believe that it will not be challenged again. It is instructive to review four incidents at Princeton and, more recently, one at Columbia. Each carries distinctive lessons.

Alger Hiss

In the still-visible shadow of McCarthyism, the student Whig-Cliosophic Society (a student organization that originated as a debating society in the colonial period) invited Alger Hiss to speak at Princeton in April 1956. There was a three-week uproar prior to the speech that involved reporters and editorial writers across the country, leading political figures, a local Catholic priest who was a strident anti-communist, and, of course, alumni. The furor is hard to believe today, but it was all too real.[16] The president at that time, Harold W. Dodds, was taken by surprise, but did not hesitate to deplore the invitation "to a convicted perjurer" as exceedingly bad judgment. Nonetheless, he insisted on supporting the right of the student group to invite Hiss, despite angry letters and impassioned pleas by friends and critics to "act" to prevent this presumed communist spy/sympathizer from coming to Princeton. And the Whig-Clio students, notwithstanding pressure from many sides, refused to rescind the invitation. The board of trustees, after a three-hour debate, joined the president in deploring the invitation but supported the decision to allow it to stand. The speech—which is said to have turned out to be quite boring—took place without incident (to the dismay of an army of reporters hoping to have something exciting to report!). The Princeton faculty and educators across the country applauded Princeton's decision to stand firm.

---

[16] For a long and colorful account of the entire history of the invitation, reactions to it, and the speech, reconsidered twenty years after the event, see John D. Fox, "The Hiss Hassle Revisited," *Princeton Alumni Weekly*, May 3, 1976; reprinted in *The Best of PAW*, 251–61.

There are three lessons. First, one should never underestimate the potential "snowballing" reaction to a controversial invitation. Second, one cannot overvalue the contribution that a key trustee can make in situations such as this one. Princeton was fortunate to have on its board Harold R. Medina, the federal court judge who had presided over the widely publicized trial of eleven leaders of the American Communist Party and who, as one university commentator put it, "stood preëminent as a foe of communist conspiracy." Medina was superbly positioned to lead the trustees in supporting the president's decision to allow the speech to proceed, which is what he did. As noted earlier (chapter 2), trustees such as Medina are often more effective in defending principles such as academic freedom than are those inside the academy. Third, alumni are more resilient and more willing to support the university, controversial decisions notwithstanding, than they are often thought to be. Donations held up well.

Governor Ross Barnett

In 1963, at a time when issues of segregation and racial injustice were high on many of our agendas, another Whig-Clio student group invited Ross Barnett, then governor of Mississippi, to speak at Princeton about education in his state. Times were calmer than they would be later, when Vietnam inflamed passions. Still, there was much irritation at the invitation and considerable pressure on students to show their displeasure by disrupting the speech. Fortunately, the event went on in an orderly way—in no small part because of strong student leadership.

There is one big lesson to be drawn from Barnett's appearance, and it has to do with the power of a well-phrased question. It is much more effective to let a speaker be impaled by his own words than to shout him down. After Barnett had stated his case for racial segregation in educational institutions, and near the end of the ensuing discussion, an undergraduate rose to ask a question. In a pronounced southern drawl, the student (who was also from Mississippi) asked: "Governor, what harm will befall me from attending classes in this university with black students?" For what seemed a very long time there was nothing but silence from the podium. Finally, Governor Barnett replied: "That's hard to say, son, that's hard to say." The meeting adjourned immediately thereafter.

Secretary Walter J. Hickel

The most serious challenge to freedom to speak—and freedom to hear—during my time at Princeton occurred in March 1970 when the secretary of the interior came at the invitation of the Princeton University Conference to participate in a discussion of environmental issues. Secretary Hickel spoke—or tried to speak—to an audience of nearly two thousand in Jadwin Gym. President Goheen introduced the secretary and was on the platform with him when a group of about seventy-five young men and women (mostly, but not all, students) began to chant, jeer, and shout insults at the speaker. As the secretary tried his best to continue to read from his text, the chanting mounted in volume: "Talk about the war!" "Talk about the war!" The secretary doggedly finished reading his script, but, thanks to the unremitting chanting, few in the audience could hear what he said. President Goheen then went to the podium, told those chanting that "This kind of interruption of a speech is in direct violation of university policy and will subject those who continue it to university discipline. You are now on warning." The chanting continued, and President Goheen concluded that it was impossible to have a question-and-answer period. He adjourned the event after apologizing to Secretary Hickel and assuring the audience that "university discipline will be exercised."

A reporter commented, "What happened on March 5 was, in effect, that a well-organized group of 60–75 persons had prevented an audience of 1,700 from hearing a speaker."[17] The protestors had succeeded in disrupting an event and the university was unable to halt the disruption, though it did succeed in identifying many of the individuals involved and charging them with violating university policy. I return shortly to this case in discussing the handling of dissent and the use of the disciplinary process. Here the lesson to be learned, and it is a painful and disturbing one, is that in an open university setting, in which there are no restrictions on entry, it is near impossible to prevent a determined and disciplined group from disrupting a speaking event. What is critical is to use any such experience to mobilize community sentiment so that it is much harder

---

[17] Landon Y. Jones, "The Hickel Heckling," *Princeton Alumni Weekly*, May 26, 1970; reprinted in *The Best of PAW*, 337. Much of the earlier description of the event is drawn from this same source.

for there to be a sequel—and to remind the campus community that one short-term "defeat" of this kind does not imply any lack of commitment to the "right to speak and the right to hear."

Dr. William Shockley

About five years after the Hickel disruption, the Whig-Cliosophic Society decided to invite Dr. William Shockley, a professor at Stanford known for thinking that genetic differences impaired the intelligence of Blacks, to participate in a debate with Roy Innis, national director of the Congress of Racial Equality. Needless to say, Dr. Shockley's views were exceedingly offensive to black people, as well as to many others, and the widely publicized difficulties that Dr. Shockley had experienced in attempting to speak on other campuses made it obvious from the outset that this was not going to be an easy situation. As president, I was determined that Shockley would be able to speak—in part so that the campus community could decide for itself if his views had substance, in part to demonstrate that the problems revealed by Hickel's appearance in 1970 were not endemic, and in part to send a message about freedom to speak on campuses that I hoped would be heard by many. My colleagues and I took pains to emphasize that

> The presence of a speaker on campus in no way denotes support
> for the speaker's views on the part of either the organization that
> issued the invitation or the University. An invitation to speak here
> carries with it no presumption that the views of the speaker are
> legitimate or valid—or even that many people will find that they
> are worth hearing.[18]

We also emphasized that the university was unwilling to delegate to anyone the power to determine who may not be heard or what may not be said on its campus.

Having learned from the Hickel heckling, a great deal of planning went into devising arrangements that would allow a good-sized audience

---

[18] This is an excerpt from a statement I issued at the time. The full text and a general account of this event can be found in *Ever the Teacher*, 13–19. Innis declined to come, but his presence or absence had little to do with the principles at issue.

to hear Shockley but that would also allow the university to monitor behavior. A number of faculty members volunteered to be present to help set a tone, one professor agreed to moderate the discussion, and the provost at the time, Sheldon Hackney (later president of Tulane and of the University of Pennsylvania), took on-the-scene responsibility for managing the event. Picketers and protestors were allowed to demonstrate outside the building where the talk took place but were not permitted to disrupt the talk. Hackney handled a bomb threat skillfully (by reporting it to the audience, so that they could decide individually whether to stay or leave, while also saying that he himself would stay), and all went smoothly. We were helped greatly by a widely shared consensus that had developed on campus—that disrupting speeches was simply wrong. We were able to demonstrate that careful planning and a clear exposition of the principles at stake make a major difference when trouble can be anticipated— that campus communities can be mobilized to defend their right to hear speakers of their choice.

The President of Iran and President Lee Bollinger at Columbia University

Dean John Coatsworth of Columbia's School of International and Public Affairs invited President Mahmoud Ahmadinejad of Iran to speak at a World Leaders Forum on September 24, 2007. There was vehement objection to this invitation to a man who had denied the Holocaust, called for the elimination of Israel as a state, imprisoned dissenters within his own country, and carried out a clandestine nuclear project in defiance of world opinion. In spite of pressures from many quarters (including from public officials who threatened to cut off funding to Columbia), President Bollinger, himself a leading expert on freedom of speech and the First Amendment, refused to rescind the invitation. In an email to the campus community before the talk, Bollinger said, "We do not honor the dishonorable when we open the public forum to their voices." Bollinger also warned Iranian officials in advance of the event that in introducing Ahmadinejad he would ask him tough questions and indicate in no uncertain terms how strongly he disagreed with Ahmadinejad on what, in Bollinger's words, "are not small matters."

Since the invitation had come from the university, President Bollinger was able to handle the event as he chose, and he more than made good on his promise to challenge Ahmadinejad when he introduced him. At one point, Bollinger said: "Mr. President, you exhibit all the signs of a petty and cruel dictator." He also called Ahmadinejad "brazenly provocative or astonishingly uneducated" for his denials of the Holocaust.

Not surprisingly, there were sharp reactions to Bollinger's introduction, which was variously described as "scathing," "belligerent," "rude," "harsh," "disrespectful," and "undignified." In the aftermath of the event, Bollinger reiterated his view that it would have been a terrible mistake not to confront Ahmadinejad as he did on issues of such consequence. Many applauded Bollinger's directness at the same time that others objected strongly to his tone and argued that he had, however inadvertently, created sympathy for a person who deserved no sympathy and made his introduction the issue. The right approach in a situation of this kind is at least partly a matter of temperament, and I do not think that I would have chosen to attack Ahmadinejad in such a direct and forceful manner. Still, whatever one's views concerning the approach taken (and it is so easy, in the aftermath of an event, to second-guess judgments of the kind Bollinger had to make), there is no denying that Columbia succeeded in allowing an enormously controversial speaker to be heard—and challenged—in a gathering that did not suffer from disruptions. It seems equally clear that the debate about the invitation, Bollinger's way of introducing the speaker, and the speech itself stimulated real thought about issues of great importance—which is of course exactly what ought to happen in a university.

We are also reminded that new challenges to the openness of a campus can occur at any time. Maintaining openness is a never-ending task, and, as this highly charged event indicates, it is often far from easy. Former attorney general Nicholas deB. Katzenbach, a longtime Princeton trustee and a faithful commentator on this manuscript, observed that this difficult situation illustrates how hard it can be to distinguish situations in which a president needs to speak out on broad issues lest his silence be misinterpreted from situations in which more restraint is called for. As Mr. Katzenbach put it: "Every rule always has—or should have—some wiggle room."

Handling Dissent and Invoking Discipline

The Value of Dissent

Annoying as dissenters can be to those in authority, there is no denying their value to a university community. In an academic setting especially, propositions of all kinds need to be challenged, for only in this way can ideas be sharpened and errors corrected. A campus free of dissent would be a boring place, and not the best environment for genuine learning. The often-strident debates over divestment, for example, were great learning opportunities for students holding diverse views, as well as for others in the campus community. In my years in Nassau Hall, I met and got to know innumerable dissenters, of all ages, stations, and positions. I learned that listening carefully, and trying to understand other points of view, paid big dividends. Policies could be improved, sometimes significantly, by taking criticisms to heart. But of course listening and agreeing are not the same thing, and very often critics left my office disappointed that I continued to disagree with them—and many no doubt left convinced that I just didn't get it. Be that as it may, engaging in genuine exchanges of opinion, and defending your own point of view, is just as necessary as patience in hearing someone out. Taking critics seriously, and responding to them thoughtfully, is a sign of respect.

My favorite dissenter was Sally Frank, a member of the Class of 1980, who was best known as a determined opponent of the all-male eating clubs. In February 1979, she filed a discrimination complaint with the New Jersey Division on Civil Rights against the three remaining all-male eating clubs. A legal battle then went on for thirteen years and ended up in the New Jersey Supreme Court. Frank eventually won her case. Combating the all-male clubs was by no means her only cause. She was also a zealous advocate of divestment and an opponent of many university policies that she regarded as too "conservative." But, to her great credit, her dissent was never personal and she always treated her opponents (including the president!) and the university itself with respect. She was extremely loyal and never failed to show up for reunions and to march with her class in the P-rade. She knew that Princeton was a great university, but she also believed that it could be much better.

Strongly criticized by some students and alumni, Frank was praised by others. In June 1990, the Alumni Council bestowed on Frank one of its annual Awards for Service to Princeton. The former secretary of health, education, and welfare, John Gardner, in a memorable turn of phrase, had warned against both "unloving critics and uncritical lovers." The Alumni Council citation correctly labeled Frank a "loving critic." I had as a colleague in the administration during Frank's time at Princeton an indefatigable free spirit who never tired of reminding me that constructive dissent is a form of loyalty. He was right, and Sally Frank exemplified his message.

But we should not be Pollyannaish and think (or pretend) that all campus dissenters are such generous spirits or as constructive. Protestors, like all others, come in many flavors. Especially at the time of Vietnam, some were just angry and destructive. As the earlier account of the "Hickel heckling" makes clear, dissent can all too easily become disruptive, and no college or university can tolerate behavior that infringes on the rights of others or threatens the essential mission of the institution. This brings us to the subject of discipline.

The Disciplinary Process

There is general agreement that colleges and universities should do everything that they can to rely on their own processes for maintaining order and, if need be, taking disciplinary actions. It is best to avoid, if at all possible, having to call police to the campus. Relying on police power can be necessary in extreme situations and should never be ruled out as a last resort. The campus cannot be seen as a sanctuary. Any recourse to outside police, however, involves ceding some degree of control over campus activities to an external authority—which can lead to other problems, including an escalation of whatever conflict caused the police to be called in the first place. I remember well a time in the late 1960s when Richard Lyman, then president of Stanford, faced such a dangerous situation on his campus that he felt that he had no recourse but to ask for the help of outside law enforcement authorities. Some conservatives applauded Lyman for his "toughness" in calling in the police. Lyman, however, rejected such plaudits and said, I believe correctly, "No one is entitled to consider the clearing of Encina Hall a victory. Any time it becomes necessary for a university to summon the police, a defeat has taken place."[19]

The ability to retain internal control in difficult situations depends heavily on both a general consensus within the university that internal control is definitely preferred over reliance on external authorities, and the presence of an effective internal process for defending the rights of the campus community. A signal contribution of the Kelley Committee at Princeton was its leadership in creating a new disciplinary body in the late 1960s, a Judicial Committee, that was charged with hearing and deciding "cases that involve alleged violations of those established rules and regulations whose violation constitutes a serious infringement of the recognized rights of members of the University community, a serious offense against the University's mission, a threat to the ability of the University to carry on its essential operations, or a substantial impairment of the common and legitimate interests of the University community."[20] The Judicial Committee had then, and has today, faculty, student, and staff members chosen by a process intended to ensure that all members are prepared to enforce established policies, and the committee's chair is appointed by the president. This committee earned its spurs when it heard the evidence against the Hickel protestors, listened to their defense of their actions, put up with a raucous atmosphere at some open hearings, and then concluded, unanimously, that all but one of the undergraduate and graduate students charged had in fact violated a clearly understood university policy and should be disciplined accordingly (with some suspended and some put on probation).[21]

The students found to have violated university policy exercised their right to appeal to the president, who had the authority to reduce penalties

[19] Lyman, *Stanford in Turmoil*, 153.

[20] See the Charter of the Council of the Princeton University Community, reprinted in the appendix to the Kelley Committee Report, and the current university Web site for a full explanation of the Judicial Committee, how it is constituted, and the procedures that it follows. One purpose of the committee was to provide a venue where members of different constituencies (e.g., undergraduate and graduate students) who were charged with violating the same policy could have their cases considered together. There are of course other judicial bodies that are concerned only with undergraduate, graduate, or faculty offenses.

[21] For a fascinating, "blow-by-blow" account of the Judicial Committee's handling of this case, see Jones, "The Hickel Heckling," 336ff.

but not to increase them. Since President Goheen had been the presiding officer at the event that was disrupted, and had issued a formal warning to the demonstrators, he recused himself and asked me, as provost, to hear the appeal in his stead. I wrote a lengthy report in which I upheld all of the main conclusions reached by the committee and all but three of the penalties. (I reduced three suspensions to probations because of a lack of clarity as to whether students who had been on probation earlier and had, as it were, "served their time," should be subject to stronger penalties because of their earlier probations.) Fortunately, the work of the Judicial Committee was widely applauded, and my handling of the appeal was also well received.

This riveting experience taught me a great deal. First of all, there is simply no substitute for having a clearly stated and well-understood set of regulations in place. The basic policy at the time of the Hickel affair, and in effect today, supports "the right to acts of peaceful dissent, protests in peaceable assembly, and orderly demonstrations which include picketing and distribution of leaflets." But it is also unambiguous in stating that "These are permitted . . . unless, or until, they disrupt regular and essential operations of the University or significantly infringe on the rights of others, particularly the right to listen to a speech or lecture. . . . It is a violation of these policies whenever any individual prevents, or willfully attempts to prevent, the orderly conduct of a University function or activity, such as lectures, meetings, ceremonies, and public events; or blocks, or willfully attempts to block, the legitimate activities of any person on the campus or in any University building or facility." The clarity of this policy, which had been endorsed officially by both the faculty and the student government, was enormously helpful. It also proved helpful to remind those who believed in civil disobedience that two of the world's greatest practitioners of this form of protest, Mahatma Gandhi and Martin Luther King, Jr., believed that individuals who chose this path had to be willing to accept the consequences.

Policies against disruption should—and generally do—apply to all members of the resident campus community, including faculty and staff as well as students. Difficult as it is to deal with student violators of such policies, it is even harder to deal with violators who are faculty members with tenure. I was fortunate in never having to adjudicate a faculty case, but the experience at Stanford with Professor H. Bruce Franklin in the early 1970s illustrates how difficult it can be to terminate faculty members, even when they are guilty of inciting outlawed conduct and endangering the lives of others. My own view—consistent with that expressed by a majority of the members of the relevant faculty committee at Stanford—is that President Lyman was wise as well as courageous in calling for Franklin's dismissal. Tenure cannot shield an individual from responsibility for gross violations of university policy.[22]

Another lesson learned from the Hickel controversy at Princeton was that disciplinary sanctions, procedures for the handling of hearings, and the adjudication of charges need to be stated as clearly as the basic rules and regulations. The Judicial Committee had been in existence only about a year when it had to contend with this highly charged case, and it was forced to make up some of its procedures as it went along. The result was an at times circus-like atmosphere that interfered with the orderly review of the charges against the protestors. The university should have been clearer in advance as to its expectations concerning decorum and the circumstances under which hearings should be closed. Similarly, the lack of precision in the rule defining the consequences of having been on probation earlier for a similar offense proved to be problematic and led me, as noted earlier, to reduce three of the penalties handed down by the Judicial Committee. This oversight was subsequently corrected so that in the future it would be understood that a repeated violation of a university policy would be treated very severely. Corrections in Judicial Committee proceedings were also made after the fact. To be sure, it would be wrong to be overly precise and legalistic in setting procedures—room has to be left for the exercise of judgment. But, to repeat, we could have done a better job of setting expectations.

A third lesson is that having the right person chair the committee can make all the difference. The Kelley Committee was wise in providing that

---

[22] See Lyman's detailed account of the long-running Franklin case (*Stanford in Turmoil*, 179 and 188ff.). See also Kennedy's account in *Academic Duty*, 132–34. Franklin was a tenured member of the English department and a self-styled radical. He was in the midst of—and really a leader of—protests that crossed the line between legal and illegal, permissible and impermissible.

the president was to appoint the chairman of the Judicial Committee, and President Goheen was equally wise in selecting as the first chairman the university's librarian, William Dix, who was widely respected and had just the right temperament. I hate to think what would have happened had a lesser person been responsible for contending—in the absence of precedents—with angry outbursts and confusion as to what was and was not proper procedure.

FIVE

Setting Academic Priorities: Annual Budgeting

Having been brought into university administration initially to reform an antiquated budgetary process in what now seems like another age, I have thought a good deal about questions of both process and principle—the two subjects of this chapter.

Process

In discussing the formation of the Priorities Committee, I have already alluded to the most important lesson I learned about process: it is invaluable to lock in one room a set of people representing different constituencies who will help you (the provost or president) confront the reality that limited resources imply the need for trade-offs. "When resources are limited, principles collide!" To be sure, the "lock-them-in-one-room" approach is easier to put into effect in a centralized place like Princeton than it is in a decentralized university.

A second lesson about process is that it is essential to have an accounting-financial record-keeping system that makes it possible to examine together all the expenditure and revenue streams needed to make thoughtful decisions about where to cut, where to spend more, and how to generate revenue. Modern computer systems make this task much easier, at least operationally, than it used to be. I still remember how hard it was, back in the late 1960s, to assemble all the information needed to understand what a particular department was actually spending; we eventually constructed something called "Form 10," which one of my colleagues thought was as important as the invention of the wheel. Not really, but it did help. There is, however, one important caveat: the argument for precision and careful analysis can be overdone. It is a mistake to apply cost-benefit analysis to everything but cost-benefit analysis itself! The opposite dangers are, however, far greater—failing to understand all the consequences of budgetary decisions.

In my later work at the Mellon Foundation, and in developing centralized resources to serve the academic community at large, I was reminded painfully of how often university budgeting procedures fail even today to capture the full effects of decisions to embrace a new electronic resource such as JSTOR (a huge electronic repository of the back files of academic journals). In the case of the library, for example, such decisions should be thought about in terms of their continuing implications for space needs and capital costs, as well as in terms of their more immediate implications for acquisition budgets. Too often, librarians would say: "Well, I don't worry about space or maintenance costs, as they are part of someone else's budget—and capital costs are years away!" Or, institutions would not recognize that adopting a systemwide resource such as ARTstor (a digital repository of art images with powerful searching and data-storing capacities) had major implications for the appropriate level of institutional investments in imaging technologies and platforms. All too often, institutions did not recognize, or take into account, the cost savings that ARTstor permitted in their slide libraries.

Given the other demands on his or her time, it is not possible for a president to be intimately involved in the details of the budgetary process, and someone else, often the provost, has to lead the process. But the president does need to be informed about the main parameters and the basic choices being made. Eventually, the president, usually with the help of the provost, needs to present a set of proposals to the trustees that they can understand and, one hopes, approve. The main contours of the budget also need to be presented to both internal constituencies (faculty, students, staff) and outside groups (alumni and often legislatures), so that the budgetary process suffers as little as possible from the "black box" problem—the inability of those not directly involved to understand how decisions are really made inside what appears to be a nontransparent "black box." This problem is complicated in many college and university settings by the presence of restricted funds and the use of fund-accounting. Contending with the horrendous financial problems faced by the University of California has not been made easier by the (unfounded) suspicions of some faculty that there is, "somewhere," a hidden pot of money that can be used to avoid painful cuts in staffing and salaries. How nice it would be if such "found money" actually existed!

Principles

A familiar conundrum is when to use across-the-board reductions in expenditures to address shortfalls. There are times when this approach may be the only practical alternative, and it has the appeal of "spreading the pain." However, I almost always avoided this approach. It is much better, I think, to be surgical in cutting budgets—preserving and, if possible, strengthening the units that will benefit most from incremental infusions of resources and cutting back, or eliminating altogether, units making lesser contributions. Rahm Emanuel, President Obama's chief of staff, is known for proclaiming that "no crisis should be wasted." I agree with him. Serious adversity can make it politically possible to reshape institutions in desirable ways. President Scott Cowen at Tulane responded to the Katrina crisis in his city by drastically pruning what he regarded as mediocre graduate programs, and taking other steps such as combining H. Sophie Newcomb College with the existing undergraduate college to create Newcomb-Tulane College. Judicious use of sharp knives can also send signals to an institution that hard choices can in fact be made.

It has become increasingly common for colleges and universities to call in outside "experts" (consulting firms and the like) to advise them on how to cut back. In general, I am highly skeptical that this is wise, even though I recognize that specialized knowledge from outside the institution can help rationalize business practices.[1] Especially in the case of decisions involving educational policies, it is people inside the institution who should know best where to cut, and they should have the courage to do what needs to be done. It is equally important to avoid temptations, in good times, to provide added resources to all programs on an across-the-board basis.

Another temptation to avoid, especially in hard times, is allowing deferred maintenance to build up in order to lessen the pain of reducing spending today on more visible and more politically sensitive parts of the budget. As the experience of many colleges and universities teaches us, deferring maintenance has extremely serious long-term consequences. There is much to be said, I think, for staying with a firm commitment to set aside a certain amount of money each year (perhaps defined as a percentage of the operating budget) for the preservation and protection of the physical plant. This is an instance in which a formulaic approach can be helpful.

A related issue, hotly debated today, is how to balance the claims of the present against the claims of the future when deciding what spending rule to apply to the endowment. There are times, I am sure, when colleges and universities have been too cautious and too mechanical in limiting the amount of endowment income that can prudently be spent currently. But I suspect that there have been many more occasions when presidents and trustees have succumbed to the temptation to harvest more endowment income in the current year than can be justified from a longer-term perspective. As the 2009 recession and attendant stock market crash teach us, it is dangerous to assume that skies will always be sunny. One practical way of handing this difficult issue is by adopting a reasonable spending rule for the long run, based on standard assumptions about likely rates of return and likely rates of inflation, but retaining the freedom to adjust the base spending rate upward in a given year if markets have been more generous over some reasonably long period of time than one had expected them to be.

Another complicated issue is how to view resources generated by a particular academic unit—especially in a decentralized university setting.

---

[1] See Bain and Company, "Achieving Operational Excellence at University of California, Berkeley, Final Diagnostic Report—Complete Version," April 2010, http://berkeley.edu/oe/phase1/phase1-full.pdf.

There is much to be said for the use of incentives, and for rewarding departments and schools that have worked hard to find the resources they need. But I am not a believer in expecting every unit to raise all of its own funds. It is intrinsically harder for some schools and departments than for others to generate revenue, and some weight needs to be given to university-wide priorities that may entail de facto subventions of some programs, using funds generated elsewhere. The "eat what you kill" motto that is applied (in part at least) in some professional firms needs to be tempered in academic settings—as it almost always is.

The provision of some amount of flexible funding can be extremely valuable. Faced with tight resource constraints and the need to make some number of important faculty appointments, my colleagues and I created a "Target of Opportunity" fund. Departments were told that they could compete for resources from this fund, and that awards would be made on the basis of the presumptive quality of proposals for new appointments that would strengthen significantly key parts of the university.

I was also extremely fortunate to have at my disposal a Presidential Discretionary Fund, which had been created well before my time in office, for the relief of distress. It was used flexibly to help students needing to get home because of an illness in the family, to ease problems for faculty and staff faced with daunting family issues, and so on. The checks were not large, but their impact was substantial. This discretionary fund also served to put a "human face" on relationships between the president's office and the campus community. As many others will attest, dollars of this kind, which can go where they are most needed, are worth many times as much as an equivalent number of dollars that has to be allocated on some formulaic basis.

A quite different point has to do with the importance of weighing carefully the long-term, symbolic impact of some kinds of cuts when setting budgets. In retrospect, I think I made a mistake when, at a time of severe budget stringency, I adhered too closely to a principle that is right in the abstract, but not under all circumstances. Let me explain. I insisted that, at the level of principle, all programs had to be "on the table" when budgetary reductions were being considered. It was wrong, I argued, to treat any budget category as "sacred." This debate quickly centered on how we should view the financial aid budget for undergraduates.

One thoughtful student on the Priorities Committee objected strongly to my insistence on asking whether we had sufficient resources to continue our unqualified commitment to meet the full financial need of all students who had been admitted (on a need-blind basis). There were other priorities, it seemed to me, including support for the library and for faculty and staff salaries, that also deserved to be respected. The student who took a contrary view argued that the long-term "cost" to Princeton and to what it stood for, by allowing itself to be seen as willing to compromise on full funding of need-based aid, was too high to accept. The university had worked long and hard to counteract the impression that it was a place for the rich, and this student believed strongly that it would be unwise to give up a continuing commitment to the policy that all admitted students from modest circumstances would be given the aid they needed to attend. If we had to shave some dollars off the library acquisition budget, or make further reductions in salary pools for faculty and staff, those actions could be reversed as soon as finances permitted. But it would be quite a different thing to equivocate on the principle that the university was genuinely open to all qualified students regardless of their means.

Of course, a continuing commitment to meeting full financial need would have been out of the question for less wealthy, less privileged institutions. But it was not out of the question for Princeton, and (I now believe) we should not have considered compromising it unless we really believed the university was in extremis—which it was not. I should have been less stubborn in refusing to see that this particular commitment to a set of values had a symbolic significance that exceeded the small savings that could have been achieved by fudging it around the edges. [2]

In addressing budgeting issues of all kinds, there is no substitute for the careful exercise of good judgment based on a clearheaded understanding

[2] To his credit, the student who felt so strongly about continuing to meet full need, and who was himself a recipient of financial aid, suggested that one way to proceed would be to substitute more loans for grants for all students receiving financial aid. That would of course have had other consequences, including both eroding implicit promises made to currently enrolled students when they were admitted (including the student who led this charge) and threatening the university's ability to attract outstanding new students who had strong financial aid offers from competing institutions. The story has a happy ending: at the proverbial eleventh hour, we were able to find enough resources to sustain the university's commitment to existing financial aid policies.

of underlying academic values and priorities. There is an ever-present need to balance carefully the arguments for staying in a "bad (resource-draining) business" because it is a core activity against the arguments for closing down programs that have become obsolete. John C. Whitehead, a very wise and experienced member of a great many for-profit and non-profit boards, has observed: "A for-profit board has an obligation to *get out* of a bad business while a nonprofit board may have an obligation to stay in, if it is to be true to its mission." It is equally important to repress tendencies to jump on every funding fad.

In sum, budgeting is every bit as much an art as it is a science, and over time I have become more and more convinced of the importance of harmonizing short-run and long-run perspectives—of making decisions as to what activities to spend money on this year in the context of a reasonably clear understanding of what choices are going to have to be made next year. I am told that in recent years, Princeton (and, I'm sure, many other colleges and universities) has made annual budgeting decisions in the context of an explicit longer-run plan that models income from endowment and other revenue streams and highlights the implications for the future of choices made today. This is a wise approach, which increases the odds of successfully harmonizing near-term goals and longer-run obligations.

SIX

Setting Academic Priorities: Strategic Decisions

In addition to constructing annual budgets, universities set academic priorities by making longer-term strategic decisions. I want now to highlight, and discuss in some detail, two major decisions Princeton made during my time in Nassau Hall: to become coeducational and (later) to invest heavily in the life sciences. Each of these decisions is replete with lessons that are, I think, transferable to other situations and many different settings. I then discuss briefly strategic decisions related to investments in graduate and professional programs before commenting more generally on the president's role in setting expectations and managing the pace of change. I defer until chapter 8 discussion of decisions made in shaping the character of the undergraduate student body, including important commitments to diversity and financial aid.

I must preface this discussion, however, by referring once again to the centralization-decentralization distinction that affects so strongly how various institutions set directions and manage their resources. As I said in chapter 1, my own direct experience has been in a highly centralized university with a single faculty and a strong concentration of power in the offices of the president and provost. In common with other colleges and universities, Princeton has a plethora of restricted funds that must be used to support the purposes for which they were given; no one can reallocate funds dedicated to, say, a professorship in English to research support for members of the engineering school. Otherwise, however, in a highly centralized setting, no department or school "owns" tuition dollars or space. In addition, all fund-raising initiatives have to be approved centrally.

As a consequence, the president, provost, and deans (acting with the guidance and approval of the trustees) have a great deal of leeway in setting directions and allocating resources—dollars, space, and "slots" (for faculty and staff appointments and graduate and undergraduate admissions). As I hope is evident throughout this chapter, this centralization model provided the levers that enabled all of the important strategic decisions that were made at Princeton during my time in and around the president's office. Centralization of authority also made it possible to align the allocation of dollars, space, and slots, thereby minimizing the risk that failure to achieve alignment will jeopardize the achievement of large objectives. I see centralization of authority as an enormous advantage.

As always, however, there are risks and offsets. Concentrating authority in this way means that it is easier to make big mistakes as well as (perhaps!) to have big wins. The premium on careful analysis obviously goes up—a seemingly small error can be very damaging. Also, centralization puts heavy burdens on the key offices and officers, including fund-raising burdens. In a decentralized structure, deans can carry major fund-raising responsibility, and the use of carefully crafted incentive structures can encourage vigorous pursuit of the goals of constituent schools and departments. Moreover, it is certainly possible (as one commentator has suggested) that the pressures and workload associated with the centralized model can take a heavy toll. Provosts—never mind presidents— are subject to "burn out." I myself favor taking such risks, if that is what they are, but they should at least be recognized.

Coeducation

The case for coeducation is so widely accepted today that it is difficult to understand how the debate at Princeton in the late 1960s could have been contentious. But it was! The nostalgic (and understandable) affection of

Princeton graduates, especially older ones, for the all-male Princeton of their day was a major obstacle to even considering such a radical move. Nonetheless, evident changes in the role of women in society, the reluctance of some of the best male candidates for admission to come to an all-male Princeton, the strongly pro-coeducation views of most faculty members, and competitive pressures from other universities considering coeducation combined to lead President Goheen to establish a campus committee charged with investigating the "desirability and feasibility" of enrolling undergraduate women. Professor Gardner Patterson, an economist who was known to be careful and dispassionate, agreed to chair the committee, whose members knew from the start that the "feasibility" part of their charge would prove to be especially daunting.

The trustees approved the establishment of the Patterson Committee, which they were promised would look hard at both the pros and cons of the question, and established a parallel committee of their own to review the Patterson Committee's analysis and conclusions. The trustee committee was chaired by Harold H. Helm. Helm was a highly respected trustee who, when asked by President Goheen to lead the committee, said, "Bob, you've got the wrong man. I'm not sure at all that I favor it." To which Goheen replied, "I'm not asking you to favor coeducation, I'm asking you to study it." Helm agreed to take the job.

An obvious lesson is that in confronting a complicated, emotional issue of this kind, which was certain to have enormous consequences however it was decided, identifying the right leadership is critical. President Goheen chose two highly regarded individuals who were known to be open-minded and perhaps even skeptical. In addition, he took pains to avoid any suggestion that he had "stacked the deck" and included on the Patterson Committee one alumnus who worked in the Development Office, was fanatically loyal to the "old Princeton," and who made clear from the start that he was against coeducation. Similarly, the trustee committee included individuals with a wide range of viewpoints. Patterson and Helm provided superb leadership during the long, arduous process of study and debate that eventually led to the enrollment of women undergraduates. One vignette speaks directly to Harold Helm's leadership of the trustee review. Harold had a brother who had also gone to Princeton and who strongly opposed coeducation—even after Harold and his committee had endorsed it. When Harold's wife, Mary Helm, was asked some years later how these two brothers, so much alike in so many ways, could end up disagreeing so strongly about the merits of coeducation, Mary replied, "Well, it's simple—Harold studied the question!"

Patterson and his committee understood full well that they were obligated not just to "study the question" but to master their subject. Much time was devoted to constructing survey instruments for different constituencies (faculty, seniors in high school, current undergraduates, alumni in the field of education), systematic efforts were made to probe the experiences of other colleges and universities, and, most important of all, countless hours were invested in modeling curricular patterns, faculty teaching responsibilities, space allocations, and every other aspect of campus life that would affect the cost of adding women students. The provost's office took main responsibility for this analytical work, and (as provost) I was fortunate to enlist an exceedingly able faculty member from the philosophy department, Paul Benacerraf, to direct much of this research. The result was a 288-page report that was widely distributed on and off campus. It was also sent to the Ford Foundation for a thorough external review. The leader of the Ford review, Joseph Kershaw, was generous in his praise: "I've never seen as conscientious and thorough an analysis of educational problems and costs anywhere. . . . It was a pioneering report." Yale later said that it had relied on the statistical analysis of the Patterson Report in making its own decision to become coeducational.

The report proved to be highly effective in correcting overly simple objections to coeducation, and especially those based on wildly exaggerated notions of what it would cost. In situations of this kind, there is no substitute for evidence based on rigorous analysis. As important as it was to underscore the reasons for believing in the educational desirability of coeducation—which proved to be relatively easy to demonstrate—it was even more important to address directly the "feasibility" part of the charge to the committee. My own conversations with trustees convinced me that the pivotal argument against coeducation would be its presumed cost. As one trustee put it, "I can see the arguments for coeducation, but we just can't afford it; it would be a terrible mistake to downgrade the educational program just to admit women." A number of trustees made the mistake of using average cost concepts to estimate the additional resources that would be required to add women students to the existing male student body.[1] In large part because of the steady buildup of the faculty in the years before coeducation, Princeton had considerable "excess capacity," and the *incremental* costs of adding one thousand women undergraduates turned out to be surprisingly modest. This was the most important finding of the Patterson Committee, and the report's cost estimates were confirmed not only by the Ford Foundation review at the time but by actual experience over the next four years.

The handling of the trustee deliberations on coeducation taught me other lessons. There was no rush to judgment, and trustees were given ample opportunity to raise questions and to express their views—as were alumni all over the country, who attended a large number of meetings to discuss the Patterson Report.[2] When it finally came time for the trustees to vote on whether coeducation was desirable "in principle," care was taken to avoid any sense that board members had to vote one way or another. The final vote was twenty-two in favor and eight opposed. The decision of President Goheen and trustee Helm *not* to press for unanimity was very wise. The presence of eight dissenters signaled to the alumni body, in particular, that there had been a real debate and no pressure to go along just to go along. To their great credit, the eight who voted against coeducation all stayed on the board and participated actively and constructively in discussions about implementation. A year or two later one of the dissenters said to me that he believed every trustee should be allowed to change one vote he had cast and that if we were given that privilege, he would certainly change his vote on coeducation.

[1]No real consideration was given to the possibility of substituting women students for men, largely because of the presumed political reaction of alumni to any reduction in the number of men students. I return to the question of the wisdom of this commitment to protect the size of the male student body—and to the dangers of making other "promises" of this kind.

[2]I led a number of these discussions and remember how surprised I was to learn that the wives of graduates were often strongly opposed to coeducation. One angry wife in San Francisco screamed at me: "If Princeton had been coeducational when my husband was there he would never have married me." I could think of no response (fortunately!).

I come now to the most important single lesson I learned from the entire process of moving from an all-male Princeton to a coeducational college: *Take as much time as needed to analyze the issues carefully and come to a considered conclusion—but once a decision has been made, put it into effect as promptly as possible. Plan carefully, then execute rapidly.* It is important both "to do it right" and "to do it now." Once the trustees had voted in principle for coeducation, in January 1969, detailed plans had to be developed for the implementation of the decision. Open questions over how to accommodate women had to be resolved and all sorts of practical decisions had to be made. Round-the-clock work by a great many people permitted what most observers thought was impossible: action by the trustees just three months later, in April 1969, on a detailed plan to enroll 130 first-year women students in the fall of 1969. The director of admissions had earlier responded to inquiries from potential women students by telling them that they could apply to enroll in the fall of 1969 as long as they understood that there was no assurance whatsoever that Princeton would be able to admit any women students. The admissions staff prepared two sets of letters to the 130 women chosen provisionally to be enrolled in the Class of 1973. One began, "Congratulations…" and the other started, "Although I wish I could convey better news. . . ." The "congratulations" letters went into the mail within an hour after the April meeting of the trustees and the second batch of letters became souvenir scratch pads.

The "forced march" nature of the preparations for coeducation was a bit frightening, since there was obviously the risk of making serious mistakes. Fortunately, the big decisions turned out to be fine—including the pivotal decision to adopt a fully coeducational model, with women to be fully integrated into the university from the start (no separate dean of women, for example). One mistake we made was to house the first group of women in a single dorm—but this error, caused in large part by practical problems associated with the room draw process, was corrected in the second year of coeducation. The Patterson Committee's projections of patterns of course enrollments were remarkably accurate.

Moving rapidly to implement the coeducation decision was highly desirable for two connected reasons. First, it avoided the problems that would otherwise have been caused by festering debate, especially among alumni, over whether the decision was really a wise one, whether it could be reversed, and so on.[3] Second, a number of us believed that it would be the women students themselves who would really sell coeducation to disgruntled alumni, and the sooner they were on campus, the sooner they could make their own case for being there. How right that judgment was! The university benefited enormously from the impressive qualifications and pioneering spirit of the first group of women students, who proved to be truly exceptional in every way. They served on many panels attended by alumni, and I will never forget one staunch opponent of coeducation saying to me after a panel discussion: "It was easy for me to be against coeducation; it is impossible for me to be against Laurie Watson" (an exceedingly appealing student from Southern California, who was good at everything and today is a leading ophthalmologist). The presence in this first coeducational class of a number of alumni daughters and granddaughters clearly helped, as did the lively participation of women students in extracurricular activities (including singing groups such as the Tigerlilies), and their immediate success on athletic playing fields as well as in the classroom.

The surprisingly widespread acceptance of the coeducation decision was also due in no small measure to the leadership of high-profile alumni who had been opposed to coeducation but who rallied to the university's cause once the decision was made. George Shultz is an excellent example.

---

[3]This was also an issue on campus. Vigorous debate was exactly what was needed prior to the trustee decision, but continuation of the debate, after the decision, would not have helped. Achieving closure with key staff members was important, and I learned firsthand how valuable a senior administrator can be when straight talk is needed. The financial vice president at the time, Ricardo Mestres, went immediately after the trustee decision to a Friday afternoon meeting with administrators, including a number of fund-raising staff who were known to be against coeducation. Mestres looked at the group and said simply: "The trustees have made a decision. Those of you who can support it strongly should come back to work on Monday." Message conveyed, meeting adjourned.

The consequences of delay are illustrated by the experience of the University of California in coping with its budget woes. In mid-September 2009, the regents discussed a budget-balancing plan in a meeting where police had to clear the room of protestors. The regents then agreed to vote on the plan when they met again, in mid-November. As one commentator observed, "This gave the opposition plenty of time to write fiery editorials and to organize protests." (See Friend, "Letter from California: Protest Studies.")

He said, in effect: "I was not in favor of this change, but the trustees obviously considered the issue carefully and came to a clear decision—let's move on!" Another one-time opponent graciously contributed a Tiger suit for a female cheerleader. It would be hard to exaggerate the outspoken and generous support of Laurance Rockefeller, a key trustee who had favored coeducation from the start. The transition to coeducation was also helped greatly by the recruitment of a number of talented women administrators and the addition to the board of trustees of several able women who themselves had prior connections to Princeton.

There were of course bumps on the road, but none that proved insurmountable. The two most serious problems were connected: (1) the need to increase the number of women undergraduates as rapidly as possible so that they would not be such a small group on what was still an overwhelmingly male campus; and (2) the perceived unfairness of the de facto quota on the number of women students that was derived from the promise not to reduce the number of male undergraduates. It was hard to defend a situation in which talented women candidates for admission were turned down because of the quota at the same time that less well-qualified men were admitted. In working through this problem, the university was helped by a growing sense that such quotas were likely to prove illegal when seen in the light of antidiscrimination statutes in New Jersey. A policy of "equal access" was adopted in the early 1970s, and the ratio of men to women students began to change rapidly. The more general lesson here is that in seeking to gain support for a controversial decision, it is wise to avoid—if at all possible—making promises that will come back to haunt you.

Investing in the Life Sciences

The second strategic decision I want to highlight was the university's major investment in the life sciences, specifically in molecular biology. Unlike coeducation, the process of arriving at the decision to make this investment, and giving effect to it, was painfully slow and in fact went on for almost a decade. Whereas the principal lessons from the coeducation decision are almost all positive, the principal lessons here are mixed. We made (I made) several misjudgments along the way, which I describe below.

First, however, some background. Historically, Princeton's great strengths in the areas of math and science have been in mathematics itself, physics, and astrophysics. Over the years, there have been a number of outstanding faculty members in chemistry and biology, but never the concentrated strength evident in math, physics, and astrophysics. By the early 1970s, it was evident to me, as well as to many others, that the intellectual breakthroughs in the life sciences were profound and that no university with high aspirations could be anything but very good in these fields.

That judgment was the easy part of the long drawn-out process of building strength in the life sciences. The hard part was figuring out exactly what to do and how to pay the bills. In retrospect, we were much too cautious for a long time—in part, in our defense, because stagflation and the economic issues of the time made resources scarce. We were also committed to making coeducation work, to improving residential life, to providing adequate fellowship support for graduate students in all fields, and to maintaining a strong financial aid program at the undergraduate level. Still, even in the face of these strongly competing priorities, we could have done better. Why didn't we?

The most serious misjudgment we made was to think that a gradual, incremental effort would work. For some years, we kept approving modest numbers of new appointments, mostly at the junior level, and making equally modest investments in renovating facilities. We enjoyed some success in identifying and attracting talented young faculty members. But we never managed to "get to scale" and the frustrations that bedeviled all of us led some of the ablest young scientists to take positions elsewhere. We kept turning over positions with little net gain.

Finally, after too many failed efforts to make sustained progress, we realized that we simply had to make a much bigger bet if we were to have any real chance to succeed. What was needed was, in combination, the creation of a new organizational unit (the molecular biology department), the recruitment of strong faculty leadership, major investments in new laboratory space, and a promise to fund more faculty positions. All of these commitments had to be made more or less simultaneously. It became abundantly clear that we couldn't build an outstanding department absent a willingness to make large upfront investments. Halfway measures had not worked—would not work.

When this light finally dawned on us, we did three things that together made a difference: (1) we stopped all recruitment of junior faculty into the existing life science departments until we could get a new organizational structure and new leadership in place; (2) we launched an all-out search for the new leadership we simply had to have; and (3) we began the process of husbanding internal funds that could be redirected to the life sciences and courting prospective donors who could make major gifts.

Finding the right leadership, which had to come from outside Princeton, was most important of all. We sought advice from many quarters, and a hero emerged: George Khoury, an exceedingly loyal Princeton alumnus who was a distinguished life scientist (member of the National Academy of Sciences, leader within the National Institutes of Health) and very knowledgeable about the relevant fields of science. Dr. Khoury, though suffering from lymphoma at the time, came to see me in Princeton to report that he knew who could lead the life sciences at Princeton. He proposed that we recruit a team of two top scientists then teaching at Stony Brook, Arnold Levine and Thomas Shenk. We cross-checked this advice with faculty already at Princeton as well as external advisors. Everyone agreed that this was an inspired idea. Khoury himself tracked down Tom Shenk (in a men's room, of all places!) when Tom was at Harvard talking about positions there and said to him: "Harvard, no. Princeton, yes."

An intense courtship followed, in which the provost (Neil L. Rudenstine), the dean of the faculty (Aaron Lemonick), and I all played central roles. We had come to understand that the stakes were so high that we simply had to mount the proverbial full-court press. Major efforts to raise money and to plan the construction of a new laboratory went on concurrently, and, in spite of periods of discouragement, we were finally successful in recruiting Levine and Shenk and in building a splendid new laboratory—thanks largely to yet another gift from Laurance Rockefeller (who was excited by the idea of naming the new laboratory for his friend Lewis Thomas, the noted cell biologist who was the president of Memorial Sloan-Kettering Cancer Center from 1973 to 1983 and a Princeton alumnus).[4] The State of New Jersey made a substantial commitment to the laboratory, and other generous donors endowed key professorships, including those held by Levine and Shenk.

This decade-long story has a happy ending, in large part because Levine and Shenk succeeded in recruiting a large number of other outstanding faculty members—including one, Shirley Tilghman, who subsequently became the nineteenth president of Princeton. Two obvious lessons are that excellent people attract excellent people and that scale (and momentum) matter greatly.

Graduate Education and Professional Schools

Strengthening the Graduate School

A recurring debate at Princeton (and at many other universities) centers on the relative weight to be given to PhD programs in the arts and sciences versus the undergraduate college. Presidents must assume a real teaching function here. In my experience, it was necessary to communicate over and over to trustees, most of whom were much more familiar with the undergraduate college than they were with the graduate school, that there is a powerful complementarity between teaching at the two levels. Business executives, in particular, are used to thinking of "product lines" and the need to avoid spending resources on relatively "unproductive" ones— witness the debates in the auto industry over the number of brands that companies like General Motors and Ford should support. It was natural for such trustees to ask why we kept spending so much money (enormous

---

[4]The timing of the construction of Lewis Thomas Laboratory was critical, because Levine and Shenk enjoyed early success attracting new faculty to Princeton and their department's temporary space was woefully inadequate. The schedule was very tight and we narrowly escaped a disaster near the end of the process when we discovered that a brick company in Utah had made the "wrong" bricks for the exterior. A trustee, John Kenefick, head of the Union Pacific Railroad, called the head of the brick company to insist that the right bricks be made immediately. Kenefick then arranged for the bricks to be shipped to Princeton on a special Union Pacific train that traveled over the Penn Central's line as well as its own. When the Union Pacific operating officer learned that the bricks had arrived safely (on a Sunday morning), he exclaimed: "Thank God!" After this experience, I had a new answer to the question: what do trustees do? A pair of the "right" bricks sits on a shelf in my office today.

amounts per student) on what seemed like esoteric PhD programs of relatively small scale when resource constraints overall were tight.

My colleagues and I had to explain carefully why it would have been impossible for Princeton to attract teachers and scholars of the caliber of Lawrence Stone in history and Val Fitch in physics without strong PhD programs. The ability of junior faculty teaching at the undergraduate level to direct good independent research and excite their students about new developments in their fields is directly dependent on their engagement with graduate students as well as undergraduates. The big lesson for me was that "continuing education" of trustees on such central points is just as necessary as continuing education of undergraduates on the need for institutional restraint when thinking about the role of a university in society. Turnover on the board (which is highly desirable if it is not overdone) means that one can never assume that next year's board will know what this year's board knows.

Even when the concept of complementarities is understood, there are of course major decisions to be made concerning how much to invest in graduate programs versus undergraduate studies. The right answer will vary over time. In the 1950s, when the country faced the need to educate far more college students than ever before, Princeton made what I am sure was a wise decision to expand its PhD programs significantly. President Goheen argued forcefully that Princeton could make a far more valuable contribution by preparing larger numbers of talented graduate students for faculty positions than it could possibly make by increasing its undergraduate enrollment modestly. That strategic decision to expand the Graduate School and to enlarge and strengthen the faculty in order to achieve this purpose later turned out, as already noted, to have been critical in allowing Princeton to become coeducational at an incremental cost that was manageable.

Over the last several decades, decisions at many universities to invest in graduate programs have been complicated enormously by the proliferation nationally of PhD programs, a process that started in the 1960s.[5]

---

[5] See William G. Bowen and Neil L. Rudenstine, *In Pursuit of the PhD* (Princeton: Princeton University Press, 1992), especially chapter 4, for a long discussion of a problem that has only worsened in the ensuing decades.

The result has been "overproduction" of PhDs in many fields. A dilemma faced by Princeton and many other institutions is that competition from new programs can cause such serious difficulties in both placement and the search for resources that it may be necessary to discontinue or cut back an existing program of good quality because there are just too many similar programs.

When I was at the Mellon Foundation I tried hard to facilitate reductions in the sizes of weaker PhD programs and in some cases their complete replacement with postdoctoral programs that would have provided similar kinds of intellectual stimulation in a much more cost-effective and system-efficient manner. Universities may often be able to attract postdoctoral students of an appreciably higher quality than PhD candidates; it is much less expensive to support the work of postdoctoral students than to mount a PhD program; and postdoctoral programs do not add to the number of new PhDs competing for a limited number of faculty appointments. Often, however, worries about loss of status if PhD programs were scaled back or phased out stood in the way of what seemed like good opportunities for rational reallocations of resources. In a recent study of undergraduate completion rates at public universities, two colleagues and I raise the question of whether some of the universities we studied have overinvested in not-very-strong PhD programs at the expense of their undergraduate programs.[6] Growing fiscal pressures on state systems may compel more universities to rethink these sensitive but important issues of resource allocation.

No Standard Professional Schools

The last strategic decision I wish to discuss is the judgment Princeton made long ago, and has regularly reconfirmed, that it should remain basically an arts and sciences university without the panoply of big-time professional schools in fields such as law, medicine, business, and education that are found at almost all research universities. This decision has been rooted

[6]See William G. Bowen, Matthew M. Chingos, and Michael S. McPherson, *Crossing the Finish Line: Completing College at America's Public Universities* (Princeton: Princeton University Press, 2009).

in the history of Princeton and also (especially in the case of a medical school) in its location in what remains a suburban community. But it has not been only a "negative" decision about what Princeton would not do. It has led to a conscious effort, over many years, to find ways in which Princeton's distinctive strengths could enable it to contribute to education in seemingly "professional" fields without giving up its concentration on the arts and sciences.

The field of law is a good example. About twenty-five years ago, the dean of the Woodrow Wilson School, Donald Stokes, considered anew whether Princeton should have a law school. His conclusion was that the country already had a number of outstanding law schools and that it wasn't clear Princeton could contribute anything special by adding another one. At the same time, Dean Stokes and his successors recognized that the Woodrow Wilson School of Public and International Affairs itself offers graduate/professional training in areas sometimes covered by law schools and that it could also collaborate with law schools such as Columbia, New York University, Stanford, and Yale in offering joint courses of study in law and public policy. There is also a relatively new program in Law and Public Affairs (LAPA) that seeks to build intellectual bridges between the university and the legal world and to coordinate law-related teaching and scholarship at Princeton. The program does not, however, attempt to provide any sort of vocational training; in that regard, it affirms and reinforces Princeton's decision not to have a law school.

Similarly, the field of business is covered in some degree by the establishment (after my time at the university) of the Bendheim Center, which offers a master's program and an undergraduate certificate in finance. Also, the School of Engineering and Applied Science has a popular department called Operations Research and Financial Engineering. It has never been evident that Princeton would make a noteworthy contribution in these areas by adding yet another standard business school. It has seemed wiser to incorporate in its regular offerings those disciplinary aspects of business schools that complement most closely teaching and research in the arts and sciences.

Serious consideration has never been given to establishing a medical school at Princeton, in part because the surrounding community lacks the urban population that normally serves as a clinical base for medical education. When the decision was made to invest heavily in molecular biology, some concern was expressed that the lack of a medical school would be a big problem. Professors Levine and Shenk never thought so and in fact argued that freedom from responsibility for managing clinical work was an advantage—especially when it was recognized that partnerships could be established with medical schools at other universities when this seemed desirable.[7] More recently, Princeton has established an integrative genomics institute and, still more recently, a neuroscience institute, both of which are relevant to medical research but are rooted in the more distinctive contributions that Princeton can make in the underlying sciences.

The lack of standard professional schools has been a major factor in allowing Princeton to operate with a single faculty and to concentrate its resources, and its energies, on the arts and sciences (as explained in discussing the "centralization" model at the start of this chapter). This "simplification," if you will, has always seemed to me to have advantages—and there is much to be said for having at least one major university in the United States with a distinct arts and sciences emphasis. At the same time, it is of course true that interactions between strong professional schools and arts and sciences faculties can be very productive in terms of both teaching and research. What may make sense for Princeton would obviously make no sense for universities such as Harvard, Ohio State, and Emory, which have long had broader mandates. The lesson, I think, is the desirability of tailoring programs of study to the particular circumstances and histories of individual universities and not assuming that because X has Y every university needs Y. The educational system at large benefits from having a variety of institutional types and models. Both faculty members and students—and presidents too!—then have a broader range of choice as to the kind of setting that will suit them best.

[7]There is a story, perhaps apocryphal, that is on point. Some years ago, there was a picture of four university presidents in an office at Stanford: Derek Bok, president of Harvard; Kingman Brewster, president of Yale; Richard Lyman, president of Stanford; and me. I alone was smiling, and a caption suggested the reason: he was the only one without a medical school.

Strategic Decision-making in General

There is, perhaps, a broader lesson to be learned from working in a university that lacks the complications (as well as, to be sure, the advantages) associated with having powerful professional schools side by side with arts and sciences departments. As I have already suggested, and want now to reëmphasize, Princeton's ability to place a small number of large bets on fields such as molecular biology was helped enormously by having a highly centralized structure in which authority, resources, and fund-raising machinery are concentrated. The large investment in the life sciences came not only from new monies raised but also from funds garnered from every nook and cranny of the university. The resulting flexibility was tremendously helpful in permitting strong actions once, and belatedly, we had learned what was required to make a determined move into a critically important field.

A different point concerns the life cycles of programs. It has become clearer and clearer to me, especially as a result of my work at the Mellon Foundation, that colleges and universities have problems getting life cycles right. They are very good at starting things but very bad at killing them off.[8] The implication is that it is critically important to be careful what you start. Over the years, I became increasingly resistant to establishing new institutionalized entities, such as centers, because they often tended to take on airs of permanence that did not always make sense. One commentator noted that in alumni publications from her undergraduate college, the announcement of a large gift always seemed to be accompanied by the establishment of a new "center." The pressures to keep an in-

[8]The University of Chicago has been perhaps the most adept research university at dealing with this problem. The uses of "committees" and "workshops" at Chicago have facilitated important teaching and research without the "permanent infrastructure" issues that are so common. Tufts has had success with an "Experimental College" structure that provides a home for curricular innovation but with no assurance that a new program will survive "incubation." I should acknowledge that eliminating entire schools or departments is devilishly difficult—as several presidents attested in commenting on this manuscript. Nor is it just hard to muster the will to act. There are often endowments restricted to certain purposes, buildings unsuited for other purposes, and potential legal and other complications (including turmoil). One president concluded, after careful study of the hypothetical case for eliminating a problematic school, "the game was not worth the candle."

frastructure functioning are strong, and the result can be ossification and inefficiency. Thus, it is necessary to be very careful in deciding when a new center or institute is really needed—as it sometimes is, especially in situations in which faculty from traditionally separate fields (such as biology-math-physics) need to collaborate more effectively in solving problems.[9]

Colleges and universities must also be careful in deciding how much to spend on programs and projects that may be somewhat peripheral to core academic activities. I have been concerned for some time about the tendency of many colleges and universities to spend money rather lavishly on projects that are less than central to the academic mission of the institution. The competition to build elegant fitness centers, student unions, and playing fields illustrates what troubles me—I see here a tendency to yield to what some have referred to as "rampant consumerism." At a time when there is so much concern about the affordability of higher education and our country's ability to find the resources needed to meet the most basic educational needs, it is especially important, I think, that relatively wealthy institutions avoid spending large amounts of money on projects that are highly visible but not necessarily fundamental to teaching and learning. To cite a specific "at home" case in point (and readers will think of many other examples from other settings), I continue to wonder whether Princeton was wise in spending $45 million, mostly from unrestricted funds, to replace Palmer football stadium with a new facility of great elegance that seems more imposing than the needs of the program can justify.[10] How an institution actually spends money, as well as sets spending priorities, sends important signals. A faculty friend at a hard-pressed public university (where a salary freeze is in place) was appalled by a de-

[9] The 2009 collapse of financial markets, with serious consequences for endowments, teaches us another lesson (for which I am indebted to Lawrence Bacow at Tufts). Funding new initiatives strictly through endowment—attractive as this approach can appear to be—carries the danger that if endowments decline sharply, institutions can be faced with the need to continue to cover the expenses of the new initiative but may now have to call on scarce general funds. There is just no substitute for raising unrestricted money and for being sure that new initiatives are really worth the potential liabilities.

[10] My general thoughts on the obligations of wealthy institutions to avoid ostentatious expenditures are reflected in the talk I gave at the installation of Morton Schapiro as president of Williams College. William G. Bowen, "The Two Faces of Wealth," Remarks at the Induction of Morton O. Schapiro as 16th President of Williams College, October 21, 2000.

cision to invite members of a search committee to a lavish dinner at the most expensive restaurant in the community. Such seemingly "small" decisions have symbolic content that it is wise to take into account. Similarly, the president has an opportunity to set a tone by avoiding ostentatious outlays and both working and living "simple."[11]

Thinking about life cycles and rhythms brings me back to the general role of the president in setting strategic directions. Several commentators emphasized that the president needs to set expectations and control the pace of change. There is a delicate balance to be struck between keeping an institution moving forward and reining in expectations that have no chance of being satisfied. There is, I have come to believe, a kind of dynamic at work in that universities push ahead vigorously for a time and then need to consolidate what they have accomplished before vigorously pushing forward again. Coeducation at Princeton unquestionably benefited from the prior buildup of the faculty in the 1950s and 1960s. The delays in making progress with the life sciences, which were costly in many ways, did have the advantage of allowing the university to accumulate the resources—and to build up the energy—needed for "the big push" that finally came.

One leader of an overseas university who has understood very well what I am trying to say here is Mamphela Ramphele, who followed Stuart Saunders as vice-chancellor of the University of Cape Town (UCT) in South Africa. Dr. Ramphele is a "force of nature," and she was certainly a change agent. She accomplished a great deal during her four years as vice-chancellor. But she was also wise enough to recognize that any university, including UCT, could only tolerate so much change in a brief period. She knew too that she would not be good at overseeing the work of consolidation. So, she stepped aside at what seemed to her the right time and made way for a successor who had a different temperament. A general lesson, by no means limited to higher education, is that some people are better at starting things and some are better at keeping the wheels turning.

[11] An amusing personal example: I have always driven inexpensive cars, and driven them for a long time. At Princeton I drove an ancient Dodge Dart for years. One morning, my colleague Tony Maruca (who understood Italian) overheard two Italian groundskeepers commenting on my driving habits. One asked: "Why do you suppose the president drives such a pile of junk?" The other speculated: "Maybe they don't pay him any better than they pay us!"

SEVEN

Building the Faculty

Building the faculty is a never-ending task, and a task that is critically important. During my time in the president's office, I devoted more time and energy to working with departments to add faculty strength than to any other activity. And it was time well spent. Over the long run, the quality of a university depends critically on what one hopes will be the ever-growing capacities of the faculty—the teaching and research abilities of individual faculty members, to be sure, but also their collegiality and commitment to the university at large.

Recruiting and Retaining Faculty

Appointing Chairs of Academic Departments

The first lesson I learned about building the faculty is the importance of identifying outstanding individuals to chair departments and then persuading them to serve in these demanding positions. In many colleges and universities, departmental chairs operate in a critical space between full-time administrators and the faculty. They are, in a nontrivial sense, both administrators and faculty members. Their leadership can make a tremendous difference. In my experience, strong department chairs are essential in recruiting and retaining the ablest faculty members, and in resisting tendencies to slide into mediocrity. It is important to avoid the temptation simply to name a truly outstanding scholar, on the often-unconscious assumption that the superb scholar will necessarily be a great judge of candidates for appointment. As one wise commentator put it in recalling the failure of a truly scholarly chair to arrest the decline of a department at his university, "Alas, the great man had a preference for likeable mediocrities."

In my view, the chair of a department needs to feel that he or she works for the president and not just for the members of the department—as essential as it is for the chair to enjoy the strong support of departmental colleagues. For this reason, I always appointed department chairs myself, after having received the best counsel I could from members of the department and key members of the administration. My practice was to write to all the faculty members in the department and ask them to send me a confidential memo explaining the main issues before the department and who they thought would provide the best leadership in addressing them. They were also encouraged to be brutally candid in telling me who they thought should *not* be appointed. I found these communications to be enormously helpful in making good appointments—and in avoiding mistakes. The memos were also invaluable guides to broader issues I needed to know about. This was a time-consuming process, but it was well worth the investment. The university provided a modest stipend to department chairs, mainly as a symbol of appreciation for what was often yeoman service; the size of the stipend has increased (properly) over time. Persuading key faculty members to serve, and sometimes to serve longer than they wished to serve, is a continuing challenge under any set of arrangements.

A question to which there is no easy answer is how long someone should chair a department. Practice varies and probably should vary. It is clearly unwise to have a "permanent" chair, but a strict limitation on years of service also seems unwise since circumstances sometimes dictate a need for considerable continuity. Some flexibility is required. But whatever the expectations concerning length of service, I am convinced that mechanically rotating faculty through the position of department chair is at least as ill advised as having chairs elected by their colleagues. Not everyone, and certainly not every great scholar and teacher, is suited for the job. An ineffective departmental leader can make it hard to accomplish positive things and can all too easily become an impediment to constructive change.

Department chairs need to report to a senior academic officer of the university, and I believe that there is real value in having a dean of the faculty who reports to the president and whose sole responsibility is faculty staffing. The alternative is to have the individual with day-to-day responsibility for faculty staffing located "down a level," perhaps reporting to the provost. This seemingly neater model has the advantage of reducing the number of direct reports to the president, but it entails a cost: it makes it more difficult to persuade a truly outstanding person to serve as the principal administrator responsible for faculty matters. In my view, this key position should have standing and visibility, which inevitably derive in considerable degree from both the person's title and his or her direct access to the president. Needless to say, under my model the dean of the faculty and the provost must work closely together, with the provost playing a critical role in deciding (with the president and others) where to invest scarce resources. But if the right people are in place, this is not difficult to achieve.

The Need for Both High Standards and a "Holistic" Approach to Recruitment

Whatever the cast of characters, and whatever the reporting relationships, everyone involved in the process of faculty recruiting needs to set the bar high—to maintain a consistently high standard. The dangers of special pleading by departmental faculty on behalf of "friends" (sometimes former graduate students) are all too real, and both department chairs and deans must be alert to this danger. It is essential to recognize that many departments, and especially specialized sections within departments, are tiny. All of Roman history, for example, may be in the hands of one or two people—and a single bad appointment can have highly detrimental effects. Larger departments can decline rapidly if even a few mediocre appointments are made. And it can take decades, not just a few years, to recover from such mistakes. This is why a rigorous process of reviewing departmental recommendations (discussed in the next section) is so important.

Departments must of course take the lead in screening potential candidates for appointment, but once top candidates have been identified, the president can sometimes play a valuable role in the recruitment process.[1] The earlier discussion of building molecular biology at Princeton illustrates this point. In that situation, the need for a high-level commitment of resources meant that the individuals being recruited had to be confident that the president and provost were solidly on board. Even when no special commitment of resources is required, a personal touch can be important. I remember a case in which an engineering department was trying to persuade a much sought-after scientist to come to Princeton— and this individual happened to care greatly about his squash game. At that time (no longer, I am sorry to say), I was a good squash player and the chair of the department asked if I would be willing to play with his candidate in the course of a campus visit. I agreed and then asked: "Am I supposed to win or to lose?" The answer was, "Win!" Fortunately, I did— and then explained to the prospective faculty member that I had many squash partners who were better players than I was, and that if he came to Princeton he could no doubt improve his game. He came—whether for that reason or not, I will never know.

Departments that are especially strong academically and especially proud of their academic standing sometimes argue that it is only the scholarly/research capacities of a candidate that matter. Academic accomplishment and academic promise are clearly of first importance, but I disagree with the proposition that no other factors should be considered. Princeton's experience in building the life sciences is relevant. That history demonstrates that leadership and collegiality are highly consequential. A visit to my office by a talented young assistant professor who had decided to leave the university made a lasting impression. He said that his working environment was so unpleasant, and personal relationships were so strained, that he just couldn't continue. "Good science," he said, "is not

[1] Some of the functions that I performed in faculty recruitment at Princeton may be the responsibility of deans in larger, more decentralized universities.

enough." Of course, universities need to welcome—and urge on—the opinionated scholar of outstanding ability who is never going to win a collegiality award.[2] I worked, more or less cheerfully, with many faculty members of this kind. But everyone cannot be like this. There has to be a core of individuals who will look out for each other and for the institution writ large.

In particular, it is essential that there be faculty members with the capacity to lead their departments, and such capacities are certainly not defined solely by having impeccable scholarly credentials.[3] The unending need to find faculty who can provide leadership, and who can be good administrators as well as fine teachers and scholars, results in part from the fact that very bright people interested in academic careers are often uninterested in such roles—and unsuited for them. This systemic pattern explains why it is critically important to seize any opportunities that present themselves to recruit talented people who can "do it all."

There is another side to this coin. There are people (fortunately, not many) who are so dysfunctional in any group context that smaller colleges and universities, in particular, need to be careful not to appoint them. Needless to say, I am *not* talking about applying any kind of social or political litmus test; nor am I arguing against the inclusion of intellectually provocative colleagues. Rather, I am talking about being aware that some individuals, because of who they are and how they relate to others, create what economists call "negative externalities"—they make everyone around them worse, rather than better. It is, as I have said, especially difficult for small places to cope with carriers of this negative externality

---

[2] One faculty friend of mine had such upsetting conversations with another faculty member that he had a card printed up that read: "On the advice of my doctor, I can discuss this subject with you no longer." He presented this card when his annoying colleague tried to extend a conversation.

[3] At one point I was looking for a new chair of a troubled department and was having no success identifying a suitable candidate. Finally, I was driven to offer the position to someone who lacked many of the qualities that a chair ought to have. I was desperate. The person in question recognized his own limitations and said to me, in the most engaging way: "Well, I will agree to do it, but both of us have to recognize that putting me in this position will be the ultimate test of 'role theory'" (the notion that people adjust their behavior to the roles that they are asked to perform). The sad conclusion to this story is that, in spite of best intentions, the individual did a truly terrible job as chair—role theory failed us.

gene. Larger universities generally find it easier to live with truly erratic and sometimes destructive behavior, but extreme cases can prove problematic even in the most sophisticated and "forgiving" contexts.

One bad appointment that I initiated was an individual who, while very bright, was so annoying to almost everyone that he succeeded in doing what no one else had been able to do: unite a disparate group of people, who now had a common enemy! This problem resolved itself because the faculty member in question kept making outrageous demands on his colleagues as well as on the university—demands that had to be, and were, rejected. In time, these "rejections" led the troublesome individual to accept an appointment elsewhere, an outcome that led to a rousing cheer from those still in place. In retrospect, I never should have recommended the appointment of this person in the first place; there were plenty of warning signs.

Dealing with the odd case can be time-consuming and draining, but it is a less fundamental challenge to building a strong faculty than creating a salary structure and a process for adjusting salaries that serve the institution well. Setting salaries is extremely important because of the obvious role compensation plays in driving decisions individuals make as to where they will work. Compensation policies and practices also have strong "signaling" effects. Too much salary differentiation within the faculty (which inevitably becomes known, even if the salaries of individuals are treated as confidential) can lead to jealousies and feelings of unfair treatment that interfere with potentially valuable collegial relations. Still, there are markets out there, and it is foolish in the extreme to believe that one can ignore such realities. Economists and engineers, doctors, lawyers, and professors of business are going to command higher salaries than faculty in most humanities fields. Refusal to recognize such differences (as British universities tried to do at one point) leads to problems of many kinds, including difficulties in attracting top people in the most competitive fields and pressures to substitute early promotions for salary adjustments.[4]

Within disciplines, too, it is necessary to recognize differences in achievement and in contributions. Incentives matter, and it is important

[4] See William G. Bowen, "University Salaries: Faculty Differentials," *Economica*, new series, 30, no. 120 (1963): 341–59.

to be able to recognize and reward truly outstanding performance. For these reasons, I have always been a strong believer in a "merit" system of compensation—albeit within a salary structure that is generally understood and accepted.[5] Needless to say, the effectiveness and credibility of a merit system depend heavily on having very good information about the performance of individual faculty members—as teachers, scholars, and contributors to the institution. Also important, I believe, is the direct involvement of faculty, both as chairs of departments recommending salary adjustments and as members of the central review committee.

Assigning department chairs responsibility for making recommendations concerning the allocation of salary pools among the senior members of a department (with the explicit understanding that these recommendations will then be reviewed carefully at a central level) encourages a culture of accountability. There is, after all, an obligation to use scarce salary dollars in ways that reflect institutional needs and priorities. Let me now qualify this line of argument in one way: when fiscal circumstances are truly grim, an across-the-board salary freeze can be an effective way of "sharing the pain," of saying "we are all in this together." But I do not believe that such a politically appealing accommodation to fiscal stress can be a long-run solution to the need to make thoughtful choices—among individuals as well as among fields.

The ability to make clear distinctions among faculty in setting salaries can also be a valuable tool in correcting the occasional mistake made in having given tenure to a person who does not live up to earlier promise. I have seen a number of situations in which communicating clearly to a

---

[5] My experience some years ago as a Denison trustee taught me that a strong emphasis on merit was easier to achieve, at least at that time, in the setting of a university such as Princeton than in a small college like Denison, where everyone knew colleagues exceedingly well. The costs to collegiality of considerable salary differentiation were greater at Denison. But I did think that the tendency to treat everyone more or less alike was overdone at Denison, and I am glad to report that today much more weight is given to "merit" in setting faculty salaries. In fact, Denison's president, Dale Knobel, reports that Denison has become comfortable with very considerable differences in salaries among individuals of the same age and experience. Another commentator with extensive experience in leading an outstanding liberal arts college (Pat McPherson, longtime president of Bryn Mawr) agrees that, over time, it has become easier to pursue a merit strategy in small college settings than it was in earlier days. As she put it, "[Merit pay] was much appreciated by the faculty you really wanted to keep."

faculty member that he or she should not expect more than minimal salary adjustments going forward led to decisions to relocate. It was sometimes possible to say simply (and respectfully) that what the person did, and liked to do, might be valued more highly at another institution. It is fairer to let someone know where he or she stands than to have ambiguity and vagueness color relationships. There is much to be said for directness and candor.

Let me conclude this discussion by recounting an experience I had with a faculty member who had just won a Nobel Prize in physics. This well-deserved recognition came at a time when a leading state university was spending lots of money recruiting top faculty, and my physicist (whom I think I can safely identify by name—Val Fitch) was told that the university seeking to recruit him would double his salary. Professor Fitch came to see me and was kind enough to begin the conversation by saying, "Don't worry, I'm not going." (We were personal friends, and that may well have encouraged him to reduce my anxiety level.) But that was not the end of the conversation. Val went on to say that his research group had real needs, and that he hoped Princeton would address them. He said (and I remember his exact words): "Excellence can't be bought, but it has to be paid for." In short, he was not going to be bribed to leave, but we had to meet his legitimate needs. I responded by saying, in effect, "Val, that's just right. We will do our best to help you and your colleagues continue to be leaders in your field, but if the time comes when we can't do that, you should leave." Professor Fitch continued to be a valuable member of the Princeton faculty until his retirement. Being willing and able to "pay for excellence" is a good way of stating the obligation of a university to someone of Fitch's caliber.

Reviewing Tenure Recommendations and Salary Proposals

As I have just said, it is critically important to have an effective process for developing recommendations for new appointments, promotions, and salary adjustments at the departmental level ("from the ground up"). An institution's ability to make consistently tough decisions at that level means that not every contentious issue has to go "all the way up the line." This exercise of discipline at lower levels is important in that it avoids putting undue pressure on the final decision-makers in every instance. But many difficult decisions do have to go all the way up the line, and I am a strong advocate of having in place a centralized process for scrutinizing and assessing departmental recommendations. The president should, ideally, play a major role in this review process (unless the university is just too large, and too decentralized, for this to be realistic). Senior administrative officers should definitely be active participants, along with elected members of the faculty. President Weiss at Lafayette reports that at his college, the president does not serve on the Promotion and Tenure Committee, which makes it hard to achieve collegiality in conducting reviews—and hard for the president to contribute in a timely way to decisions on important and complicated cases.

My own experience was with a process at Princeton that I thought worked extraordinarily well. The key organizational entity was the long-established faculty Advisory Committee on Appointments and Advancements, widely known colloquially as "the Committee of Three" because it originally had three faculty members. Today it has six faculty members (all full professors, with at least one from each of the four divisions of the university, and always at least two department chairs). The faculty members are elected by their colleagues from a carefully prepared slate of candidates. The president chairs the committee, the provost and three other senior academic officers meet with it, and the dean of the faculty is its secretary and the person responsible for its smooth functioning. The committee advises the president on the appointment of professors and associate professors, on all promotions to tenure, and on salary recommendations.

In my more than twenty years of experience with this committee (as provost and then as president), I was never once disappointed in it. The elected faculty members and administrative participants met together so often (in those days generally after dinner and always in the same room in Nassau Hall) that it was natural for them to "bond." After extensive deliberation, the committee almost always came to unanimous judgments about what they believed to be the right course of action. As its formal name indicates, the committee is advisory to the president, who is not bound by its conclusions, but I cannot recall a single occasion when I had to overturn a recommendation of the faculty members on the committee. The fact that the president chairs the committee, and the dean of the faculty serves as its highly active secretary, helps explain the lack of any faculty-administration split.

Two principles are worth highlighting.

First, recommendations for new appointments or promotions to tenure have to be judged in the context of departmental and university needs, not just in terms of the "absolute" merits of the candidate. If a department already has a relatively young tenured member in twentieth-century American history, for example, it may not make sense to award tenure to someone else of roughly the same age who has the same interests. Complaints about unfairness ("look at how good the candidate is") cannot override the need to allocate resources responsibly.

An even more important principle is the desirability of resolving doubts or uncertainties against the candidate, hard-hearted as this may seem. A wise dean of the faculty used to say, "doubts increase." By this he meant that if the committee is at all uncertain about a candidate's quality or prospects, the odds are high that such "doubts" will grow over time. That is a lesson I learned over and over again: doubts increase. Difficult as it is to deny a promotion to someone colleagues like and think will get better over time, it is wiser, as a general rule, to just say "no" if there are reservations. A related proposition is that if a department already contains several mediocre faculty members, it is almost always a mistake to add someone else who is not really excellent—even if the individual is better than most current members of the department.[6]

This model of the review process depends heavily on having at its core a set of highly respected faculty from across all divisions of the university who will apply a demanding standard in evaluating every departmental recommendation. To be sure, this means that the committee will need to be assiduous in collecting detailed information about a candidate from

[6] I remember one extreme case in which the committee turned down a recommendation from a not-very-strong department even though the department insisted that the candidate was better than anyone now in it. "Perhaps," was the response, "but not good enough."

outstanding scholars at other universities who work in the same field. Such discipline-specific, subject-specific assessments are essential. In the Princeton context, the dean of the faculty was responsible for assembling such information, and the dean made a practice of always asking experts to give him the names of others who might be consulted, and especially others who might have a different point of view. It is a mistake to rely solely on testimony from outside referees suggested by the candidate or the candidate's department. The committee is then responsible for reviewing all the evidence and, if need be, asking the dean to learn still more about the views of one referee or another, often via telephone calls (since scholars seem increasingly reluctant to "tell hard truths" in writing).

This is a time-consuming process, but it can produce, and in my experience often did produce, a highly nuanced picture of an individual's strengths and weaknesses. There is much to be said for having a single, experienced, respected set of faculty members from all across the university weighing evidence and discussing a case among themselves and with the president and deans before a conclusion is reached. The active participation of what Quakers would call a "weighty group" gave legitimacy to the process and usually succeeded in persuading disappointed individuals and departments to accept the outcome, whatever it was.

There are, to be sure, other models, including some in which the faculty participants in the review process are chosen in part because of some familiarity with the candidate's field of study and thus differ from one tenure case to another. Having detailed disciplinary knowledge is of course essential. But this model raises the very real risk that standards will differ from field to field (and thus from case to case), and it also deprives the review process of respected faculty colleagues who have had experience in evaluating many recommendations in many fields. As I said earlier, I think that the specialized knowledge about disciplines and fields that is clearly needed for informed conclusions can be obtained from individuals who are not themselves members of the review committee.

Let me now comment briefly on the role of trustees in reviewing the president's tenure recommendations. There is a simple but critically important distinction to be drawn: the trustees have both the right and the responsibility to review carefully the *process* by which recommendations are developed, to satisfy themselves that it is both fair and well suited to produce good recommendations. But trustees should refrain from attempting to make their own judgments on the qualifications of particular candidates. That is the job of the faculty, the deans, and the president. If, over time, the trustees become skeptical that the president is handling this key responsibility well, the answer is to get another president, not to second-guess the one in office. Candidates for promotion and individuals being recruited from outside the university need to be confident that their cases will be handled professionally and not be subject to idiosyncratic judgments of trustees. Saul Kripke is a distinguished philosopher who was recruited from Rockefeller University to come to Princeton when I was president. Saul felt that he had to resign his current position before we could formally appoint him, and he expressed some nervousness to me when he said: "But what if the trustees reject your recommendation that I be appointed?" My response: "If that happens, both of us will be looking for jobs."

Trustees also need to understand that their responsibility is a collective one, and that individual members of the board should refrain from criticizing personnel decisions that they dislike. After I left Princeton, a case arose in which a prominent and politically active trustee publicly expressed extreme displeasure at the presence on the faculty of Professor Peter Singer, a distinguished philosopher who was controversial because of his views concerning subjects such as euthanasia. The trustee went so far as to say publicly that he would give no more money to Princeton as long as Singer was on the faculty. In my view, this trustee's behavior was beyond the pale, and I was pleased that the board of trustees, acting collectively, issued a public rebuke.

Faculty Diversity

A major challenge for all of higher education is to increase the diversity of the faculty, measured along many dimensions but especially gender and race. This is a subject of great complexity that merits (and has often received) book-length treatment. Here I can only highlight a few lessons I learned in seeking to increase diversity—which proved appreciably easier to do in the case of gender than in the case of underrepresented minorities.

It almost goes without saying that universities have to find ways to include on the faculty larger numbers of individuals from historically underrepresented groups. The reasons are well known and need not be recounted here. It is, however, far easier to agree on the importance of the objective than it is to make as much progress as we need to make. The most fundamental lesson to be learned in this area is that the underlying pools of candidates limit, sometimes dramatically, what can be accomplished, especially in some fields and over short periods of time. It is necessary to be realistic in recognizing this fact of life. The key to making long-term progress in achieving greater faculty diversity is to increase the number of well-qualified minority graduates of PhD programs. My frustration in dealing with this problem at Princeton led me to create the MMUF program as my first initiative at the Mellon Foundation. Originally called the Mellon Minority Undergraduate Fellowship program, and now called the Mellon Mays Undergraduate Fellowship program, its basic purpose from the outset was to encourage more highly talented minority students to pursue PhDs and then enter academic life. The program is very much alive and well today and has already produced over three hundred PhDs, with many more to come.[7]

Still, as we are all aware, there is much yet to be done. An MIT report issued in 2010 documents in great detail how difficult it continues to be for a great university like the Massachusetts Institute of Technology to increase the numbers of faculty from underrepresented minority groups.[8] Required is both impatience—we must work ever harder on this daunting problem—and patience—since, even with the best intentions and the most effective programs, progress will be slow.

Individual examples continue to help me understand why these efforts are so important. A Princeton faculty member in the Spanish and Portuguese Languages and Cultures department, Arcadio Díaz-Quiñones,

---

[7] For more information about the MMUF program, please visit the Web site www.mmuf.org.

[8] "Report on the Initiative for Faculty Race and Diversity," Massachusetts Institute of Technology, January 14, 2010. Scott Jaschik, "Race and Merit at MIT," *Inside Higher Ed*, January 15, 2010, www.insidehighered.com/news/2010/01/15/mit.

played an absolutely critical role in helping a talented undergraduate from South America, who was an undocumented immigrant, overcome difficulties of all kinds and go on to graduate Phi Beta Kappa, attend Harvard Medical School, and work today as a cardiac surgeon. The student in question, Harold Fernandez, needed desperately to find a faculty member he could trust to understand his plight and help him. I hate to think what would have happened to Harold had Arcadio not been on the scene.[9]

[9] This inspiring story was recounted in the *New York Times Magazine*, January 3, 2010, ED28, and is the subject of a forthcoming book by Harold Fernandez and Joseph Berger.

EIGHT

Undergraduates: Admissions, Financial Aid, and Inclusiveness

Strategic decisions of many kinds have to be made in crafting an undergraduate class and in creating a structure within which students can relate to each other and to the university at large. There was a time when colleges and universities thought about admissions mainly in terms of enrolling enough students of reasonable quality to allow the place to function. Similarly, concern with residential life was focused on creating a campus setting that would be attractive to potential students and otherwise relatively unproblematic (free of riots). "Selective" colleges and universities were not all that selective until after the end of World War II.[1] One major strategic decision in the postwar period at most historically all-male colleges and universities was to admit women (the path to coeducation at Princeton has already been discussed). Another decision was to give up the simply indefensible "Jewish quotas" that were an appalling part of the history of many colleges and universities.[2]

[1] For an excellent discussion of the factors that led to the "nationalization" of the marketplace for student talent and to the increase in stratification, see Caroline M. Hoxby, "The Changing Selectivity of American Colleges," Working Paper 15446, NBER Working Paper Series October 2009, http://www.nber.org/papers/w15446.

[2] See Jerome Karabel, *The Chosen: The Hidden History of Admission and Exclusion at Harvard, Yale, and Princeton* (Boston: Houghton Mifflin, 2005).

Diversity and Financial Aid

Most colleges have provided scholarship aid to needy students for a long time. But, beginning in the mid-1960s, there has been a growing awareness of the educational value of diversity—as well as the obligation of colleges and universities to foster social mobility by making special efforts to enroll talented students from every background. Many institutions separated admissions decisions from financial aid by adopting need-blind admissions policies, and those colleges and universities that had the requisite resources sought to meet the full need of all students who qualified for admission. This was always for me, as for many others, a very high priority. In her inaugural remarks as president of the University of Pennsylvania, Amy Gutmann proposed a "Penn Compact" that had a central premise: "In a democracy and at great universities, diversity and excellence go together. Keeping them together requires access based on talent, not income or race."[3]

I agree. Following the tense budget debates of the 1970s, when I now believe that I was more willing to consider compromising the principle of meeting full need than I should have been (see the discussion in chapter 5), Princeton identified strengthening its scholarship program as a top strategic priority. Whenever I had a choice, I directed potentially unrestricted gifts to long-term support of the financial aid program, and Princeton was so successful in these fund-raising efforts that today it has (I believe) more endowment restricted to undergraduate financial aid, relative to its requirements, than any other college or university.

Prior to the decision of the Justice Department to bring antitrust actions against the Ivies and other institutions that participated in "overlap" meetings designed to exchange information and avoid bidding wars for potential students (a decision by the Justice Department that I continue to think was very unwise), there was a widely shared effort to make the best, most efficient use of scarce financial aid dollars by concentrating them on the neediest students. Subsequently, there has been some erosion of this principle, and the growth of differential financial aid

[3] Dr. Amy Gutmann, Inaugural Address, University of Pennsylvania, October 15, 2004, https://secure.www.upenn.edu/secretary/inauguration/speech.html.

calculations and financial aid "packaging." Here is a lesson for all of us: in the right circumstances, sensible (and transparent) collaboration among educational institutions to advance the common good makes all kinds of sense.[4]

In recent years there has been a tendency to replace loans with grants, especially for students from modest circumstances. Everyone should applaud this effort to reduce financial worries for needy students, but there are legitimate questions concerning how far up the income scale such policies should apply. A worry is that more affluent institutions will put great pressure on their less affluent competitors to divert dollars badly needed for other purposes to provide "rich" financial aid packages for students who are from families well above the normal definition of "middle income." Individual students at resource-rich universities are direct beneficiaries of the expensive education that they receive, and I have always believed that it is fair to expect some reasonable degree of family contribution and some willingness on the part of students to take out loans—as long as the amounts are not too burdensome.

Next, a "mea culpa" on the subject of competition for students and financial aid. The Ivy League has long had a strict policy precluding any use of merit aid—which I have always supported strongly. Nonetheless, I tried to get an "edge" for Princeton by proposing that we offer honorary research awards to outstanding applicants—providing them with modest research allowances that would not, however, affect either their obligations to pay tuition or their financial aid packages. Other Ivy presidents objected, saying that while technically this program did not contradict the "need-only" financial aid policy of the Ivies, it did have a merit aid feel to it. They were right, and I abandoned this effort. Temptations to be "too clever by half" should be resisted.

There is also a broader lesson for all of higher education. Easy as it is to understand why individual colleges and universities want to do all they can to attract top students, liberal use of merit aid can be highly prob-

---

[4] I testified on behalf of the overlap concept when MIT continued to oppose the position of the Justice Department—but other institutions had already entered into consent agreements that, de facto, ended the overlap meetings. Affidavit of William G. Bowen, Civil Action No. 91-CV-3274, U.S. District Court for the Eastern District of Pennsylvania, April 29, 1992.

lematic for the overall system of higher education. First, such policies may not be very effective if competitor institutions match offers. The more fundamental point was made crisply by Lawrence Bacow in a statement to the Commission on the Future of Higher Education: "It is far from clear to me how society is better off when scarce financial aid resources are diverted from the neediest students to those who are not needy by any measure, simply to redistribute high-scoring students among our institutions."[5] A moral of this story is that, in my view, presidents should try hard to keep their competitive instincts under control when it comes to awarding financial aid. We should also recognize, however, that it is far easier for the strongest and most selective institutions (such as Princeton) to take the high ground in opposing merit aid than it is for institutions that have to struggle harder to recruit excellent students. Thus, I am sympathetic to the efforts of places like Denison to use a limited amount of scholarship money to attract particularly strong students who improve the academic program on campus for everyone. It is a matter of balance and of respecting differences in circumstances.

Affirmative Action and Race

Against this background, let me turn now to admissions policies related to a particularly important aspect of diversity: the recruitment of minority students. Putting coeducation to one side (and I return later in this chapter to religious divides), the most consequential action affecting admissions and undergraduate student life in American higher education since World War II was the decision by almost all selective colleges and universities to recruit—aggressively—many more minority students than they

[5] Reprinted in the February 8, 2010, release issued by Tufts announcing President Bacow's decision to step down from the Tufts presidency in 2011. See http://president.tufts.edu/1262786793854/Pres-Page-pres2w_1265032241220.html. My colleagues and I commented on this subject at length in our book on graduation rates at public universities (Bowen, Chingos, and McPherson, *Crossing the Finish Line*, especially chapters 9 and 12). We cite a College Board study showing that only 44 percent of grant aid dollars at public four-year institutions went to students who had financial need (231). Nearly 40 percent went to nonneed students, and 18 percent went to recruited athletes (including a number with need). Many private colleges and universities of course also provide merit aid.

had traditionally enrolled. I spent a great deal of time pursuing this goal from the 1960s on, and issues of race have continued to be compelling to me personally. Like many others, I have long believed that confronting what Glenn Loury called "America's unlovely racial history" is profoundly important, not just to higher education but to the health of our entire society.

Over time it has become increasingly evident that the educational quality of an institution depends on the mix of its students as well as on the quality of the individuals enrolled. Students really do learn from each other—this is far more than a cliché. The demonstrations and seemingly endless debates over divestment in which I participated had a major educational effect on students of all races and backgrounds—which, I confess, it is far easier for me to appreciate in retrospect than it was at the time! In the course of writing a book on race-sensitive admissions, Derek Bok and I collected vignettes from students in the cohorts we studied that attest to these educational effects. I reproduce two of them here.[6]

A white woman in the '89 cohort at Wellesley:

During the Rodney King riots, a lot of the black students, including my roommate, really wanted to go to Ethos (the black women's house). And she looked at me and said: "I can't look at white people right now. I'm sorry, I like you, I love you, and you're my roommate, you're my friend, but I need to absent myself." So she went over to this house with her African American friends. And at the time it took me a lot of time to understand it and I think a lot of the white students were bewildered. And we had a speakout in the Senate. That was when I began to understand that sometimes you have to go back to people who are like you to gain strength to deal with the world. It made sense.

[6] William G. Bowen and Derek Bok, *The Shape of the River: Long-Term Consequences of Considering Race in College and University Admissions* (Princeton: Princeton University Press, 1998), 239, 254. For a broader, comprehensive analysis of the educational value of diversity, see Patricia Gurin, with Eric L. Dey, Gerald Gurin, and Sylvia Hurtado, "The Educational Value of Diversity," http://141.211.86.200/pdf/0472113070-ch3.pdf.

A black member of the '76 cohort at the University of Michigan:

I grew up in Detroit, and I really had no contact with any white people at all. My first roommate as a freshman was a white guy and we became very good friends, which was a surprise to me. . . . He was just a decent guy. Now I'm the only black guy in this office, and I don't have any problem with that. But that goes back to my having had this guy as a roommate.

As Justice Sandra Day O'Connor made clear in her opinions on the University of Michigan affirmative action cases, there are other reasons besides the educational value of diversity for favoring a "holistic" consideration of race in admissions (sans quotas and the mechanical assignment of bonus points). The country needs the talent present in its minority population: the preparation of larger numbers of well-educated minority students for leadership positions in the professions, business, academia, the military, and government is itself a strong reason for adopting race-sensitive admissions policies. Moreover, the social fabric of the country requires, in Justice O'Connor's words, that "the path to leadership be *visibly open* to talented individuals of every race and ethnicity [my emphasis]."[7]

This is an issue of public policy, as well as university policy, that a university president has not only the right but the obligation to address. A university simply has to have an admissions policy (as it does not have to have a policy on labor practices in the textile industry—refer back to the discussion of the proposed boycott of J. P. Stevens in chapter 4), and those of us in universities are better positioned to discuss the reasons why race-sensitive admissions matters than are others who lack our experience. When a national issue is central to the functioning of the university itself, the presumption against direct university involvement is overturned. I wrote an early piece on this subject for the *Princeton Alumni Weekly*[8] that was cited several times by Justice Powell in his *Bakke* decision, and Derek

---

[7] *Grutter v. Bollinger et al.*, 539 U.S. 306 (2003) at 332.

[8] William G. Bowen, "Admissions and the Relevance of Race," *Princeton Alumni Weekly*, September 26, 1977.

Bok and I were gratified that *The Shape of the River* was quoted exten-
sively by Justice O'Connor in her opinions in the Michigan cases. There
are times to speak out, just as there are times to hold back.

In the early years of minority recruitment at Princeton, I was reluctant to examine closely or publish data on educational outcomes for
minority students—because of a fear that the results would "look bad"
or be misinterpreted. That was a mistake on my part. In fact, as the later
findings in *The Shape of the River* demonstrated, minority students at selective colleges and universities (including Princeton) did just fine. But
in any case, however they had performed, it would have been better to
look directly at outcomes, and to acknowledge shortcomings when
they were found, than to suggest by silence that maybe there really was
something wrong. I now believe that accountability requires that educational outcomes of all kinds, sensitive or not, be examined and discussed.
Daytime realities are almost never as bad as nightmares. The extensive
public discussion that followed the publication of *The Shape of the River*
also taught me that unjustified criticisms of policies (based generally
on lack of knowledge) had a chilling effect on black students. Herewith
another vignette, based on a conversation I had with a recent graduate
following a speech in Washington:[9]

> After a presentation to the American Council on Education, a young
> African American woman came up to me and introduced herself.
> She had been an undergraduate at Harvard in the mid-1980s, and
> she reported that she had studied the *River* carefully and had found
> it, in her words, "liberating." She went on to say: "I guess I have been
> walking around with a kind of cloud over my head, which I didn't
> really understand was there, and it's gone now. . . . We did pretty
> well, didn't we?" "Yes," I responded, "You did very well indeed." She
> nodded and added, with emphasis, "Thank you. I'm ready, now, to
> stand up and fight!"

[9] Bowen and Bok, introduction to the paperback edition of *The Shape of the River*, xxxiii.

Among the many other lessons that could be drawn from experiences with race and admissions, let me mention just two: (1) the need to do more than simply admit minority students; and (2) the need to achieve a critical mass of such students.

When we started aggressive recruitment of minority students, many of us, at Princeton and elsewhere, did not appreciate the extent of the adjustment problems that would confront some of these students when they entered what were for many strange and even threatening settings. Some of us foolishly extrapolated from long experience in admitting white students from modest circumstances, including children of ministers like my predecessor Robert F. Goheen. But while students like Bob Goheen had little money, they were rich in the cultural capital prized by elite universities; they also generally came from academically demanding secondary schools that were sending classmates and friends to Princeton. It was far more difficult to find ways to make many minority students feel "unselfconsciously included"—a wonderful formulation by Jerome Davis '71, of what we wanted to achieve. Senior leadership was also critical, and Princeton was fortunate to recruit an experienced educator, Carl Fields, who worked tirelessly to ease adjustment problems.[10]

The lack for many years of a "critical mass" of minority students was a closely related problem. Many people, inside and outside academia, have learned a great deal from those early experiences, and it was gratifying to see Justice O'Connor's explicit endorsement of the desirability of enrolling more than a token number of minority students.[11] Recent research, sparked by the pioneering studies of Claude Steele, has demonstrated

[10] See Carl Fields's own account of his activities: "The Black Arrival at Princeton," *Princeton Alumni Weekly*, April 18 and 25, 1977; reprinted in *The Best of the PAW*, 327–35. See also the 1997 video by two alumni, Melvin McCray and Calvin Norman, *Looking Back: Reflections of Black Princeton Alumni*, which is based on interviews with black students describing how some of them felt about their experiences. There are also two perceptive accounts by Jerome Davis: "A New Day for Black and White," *Princeton Alumni Weekly*, October 21, 1969; and "Statement Written on Behalf of ABC (Association of Black Collegians) for the Princeton University Yearbook *Bric*," 1970. Davis was one of a number of extraordinary African American students who were at Princeton during the most challenging years. He was the founder and leader of a highly influential group called the Association of Black Princeton Alumni (ABPA) that provided leadership for students and alumni alike. Davis also assembled materials (to be deposited in the Princeton Archive) that provide rich insights into the varied experiences of a wide range of black students at Princeton.

[11] *Grutter*, 539 U.S. at 343.

powerfully how important critical mass is in helping minority students cope with stereotype threat.[12] As the number of minority students, and especially African American students, increased, it was easy to see the advantages of critical mass. African American students felt much less need to "speak for" other African American students, an impossible task in any case because of the inevitable differences in viewpoints within as well as across all groups. Racial discomfort is in no way gone from campus settings, but it is encouraging to see how much more comfortable many minority students now feel at "their" universities—as evidenced by their participation in reunions and the active role many graduates play in encouraging prospective students to apply.

Socioeconomic Status

Most universities recognize that they should be open to students from all backgrounds—and that, indeed, some special effort should be made to enroll students from modest circumstances. Need-blind admissions and a policy of providing enough financial aid to meet students' full need are the primary tools that have been used at Princeton and other resource-rich institutions to achieve this objective. During my years in the president's office, I thought that these policies were indeed effective in enrolling students from all backgrounds and that the admissions office was giving some special consideration to students who had overcome hardships to qualify for admission. After leaving the university I learned that this judgment (really this optimistic assumption) had been right only in part.

Research that a group of us carried out on admissions policies at a range of academically selective colleges and universities demonstrated conclusively that large admissions advantages were given to recruited athletes, students from underrepresented minority groups, and legacies—but not to low-income or first-generation applicants. (Admissions advantages

---

[12]See Claude Steele, *Whistling Vivaldi and Other Clues to How Stereotypes Affect Us* (New York: W. W. Norton, 2010), especially 137ff. Of course, stereotype threat affects groups other than black students. (Justice O'Connor herself said how much more comfortable she was on the Supreme Court after a second woman was appointed.) See also vignettes in *The Shape of the River* for actual examples of how stereotyping affected minority students in our study.

are measured by the probability that a member of the group in question will be admitted, compared to the equivalent probability for "students-at-large" with similar qualifications.) The study found that applicants from low socioeconomic status (SES) backgrounds, whether defined by family income or parental education, got essentially no break in the admissions process. This finding stands in sharp contrast to the published assertions by most selective institutions that they do pay special attention to students from disadvantaged backgrounds.[13]

Those of us who did the study were surprised by this finding, but we did not suggest that the odd disjunction between fact and assertion was due to any tendency to be disingenuous—I was, after all, one of the people who had claimed that low-SES students were in fact getting some admissions advantage! Rather, we surmised that the disjunction was attributable to a lack of good data, an inclination to rely on anecdotes (known cases of some students from poor families who were admitted in spite of less-than-stellar credentials), the admission of some number of "development" candidates, and the role of "champions" in the admission process.[14]

[13] See William G. Bowen, Martin A. Kurzweil, and Eugene M. Tobin, *Equity and Excellence in American Higher Education* (Charlottesville: University of Virginia Press, 2005), especially chapter 7, for a long discussion of admissions preferences. There is, I think, no formula that can dictate the amount of admissions preference that should be given to any group; in highly selective institutions, admissions preferences of all kinds carry with them opportunity costs since some exceptionally well qualified candidates will be turned away.

[14] "Development" candidates are applicants from families that are thought to have the potential to help the institution financially. I recognize the arguments in favor of giving some preference to a limited number of these candidates, even as we also have to acknowledge that the existence of this class of admissions advantages obviously works against a desire to raise admissions probabilities for low-SES students. (See the discussion in *Equity and Excellence* referenced in the previous note.) As one commentator observed, those of us associated with selective institutions that admit development candidates should not be too sanctimonious in criticizing other institutions for failing to be sufficiently "pure" in their admissions and financial aid decisions.

A more important explanation for the finding showing the lack of a relationship between admissions probabilities and SES is the role of "champions" in the admissions process. Another president of a highly selective university who was as surprised as I was by the empirical findings explained the results in terms of a combination of lack of the right data (to calculate an admissions advantage it is necessary to know the family backgrounds of *all* applicants, and such data are hard to assemble) and the role of "champions" in the selection process. The president who offered this analysis of "lack of champions" for low-SES students had observed the admissions process at his own university and noted that when the admissions staff considered an outstanding soccer player, it was as if "lights went on in the room"—everyone knew that the coach and AD were in

It is relevant, and revealing, that a Harvard economics professor, Christopher Avery, and his coauthors found that presidents were also unaware of how much of an admissions advantage was in fact being given to early action and early decision applicants. The same set of factors was at work: lack of the right data, lack of knowledge of how to analyze the data, and too much of a tendency to believe what one wants to believe.[15] A big takeaway for me is that presidents need to be careful to avoid making claims not supported by rigorous analysis of the relevant data. Let me re-ëmphasize that I was as guilty as other presidents of not understanding this. Let me also add that I am highly skeptical of the value of both early action and early decision programs—which inevitably favor applicants who "know a lot" and are well connected. Whatever modest competitive advantage an institution can gain by employing such programs has to be balanced against potential costs of other kinds, including unfairness and unintended effects on secondary school programs.

It is also easy to fall into the trap of assuming that sensitive admissions policies and generous financial aid will suffice to overcome the vulner-abilities felt by many students from low-income families who attend in-stitutions that attract large numbers of students from privileged back-grounds. There is a strong correlation between socioeconomic status and outcomes of all kinds (including graduation rates and time-to-degree) that persists in both public and private institutions no matter how many other factors are taken into account.[16] The implication I draw is that educational institutions of all kinds need to be aware of the continuing advantages as-sociated with coming from an affluent, well-educated family, and to do as much as they can to allow students from modest circumstances to enjoy equivalent opportunities to benefit fully from college.

---

effect watching closely and cheering the candidate on. Similarly, advocates for minority students were vocal champions for their candidates, as was a person watching out for "legacy" candidates. Representatives of athletic interests, minority recruitment, and legacy candidates were all present in spirit and sometimes in person. But, the president went on, when an "ordinary" candidate from modest circumstances was considered, the process just moved right on without anyone making a special plea. (See *Equity and Excellence*, 175–76.)

[15] See Christopher Avery, Andrew Fairbanks, and Richard Zeckhauser, *The Early Admissions Game: Joining the Elite* (Cambridge: President and Fellows of Harvard College, 2003).

[16] See Bowen, Chingos, and McPherson, *Crossing the Finish Line*, for evidence.

Athletic Recruitment

Reluctant as I am to reenter this treacherous territory,[17] it would be wrong to fail to comment here on some of the lessons I learned through experiences with the recruitment of athletes. In company with most other presidents, I was at least dimly aware that there were problems with the ever-increasing intensity of athletic recruitment, even for athletes in the so-called minor sports, and even in colleges and universities without athletic scholarships and big-time basketball and football programs. Many of these colleges and universities admit large numbers of recruited athletes whose academic credentials do not measure up to those of their fellow students (sometimes 20 percent of the entering class at small colleges). In our study, recruited athletes were found to have received an average admissions advantage of more than 30 percentage points—which means that if a "student-at-large" with a given set of credentials had a 25 percent chance of being admitted, a recruited athlete with the same credentials had a 55 percent chance of admission. As a consequence, the institution incurs a large "opportunity cost" as a result of its failure to admit a number of highly qualified applicants. And in fact, the problem is more serious than this. Evidence indicates that, in general, recruited athletes "underperform"—that is, they do even less well academically than one would expect them to do on the basis of their (below average) entering credentials. A far from inconsequential number of these students fail to take full advantage of the educational opportunities that they are offered. Research that Sarah Levin and I carried out demonstrates that it is "selection effects," not "treatment effects," that are primarily responsible for these outcomes. That is, the root of the problem is not so much the time athletes spend practicing and playing (treatment effects) as it is the recruitment process itself, and

[17] With colleagues, I have written two books on the subject of intercollegiate athletics and educational values that criticize many current policies and practices. See Shulman and Bowen, *The Game of Life: College Sports and Educational Values,* and William G. Bowen and Sarah A. Levin, *Reclaiming the Game* (Princeton: Princeton University Press, 2003). To this day, I wear protective garb when meeting with athletic directors!

the interests and motivations of different sets of students captured by it (selection effects).[18]

One of the mistakes I made in attempting to address the problem of academic standards for recruited athletes in the Ivy League was to put too much emphasis on the presumed curative power of an "academic index" that focused on the academic qualifications of athletes when they are admitted. What is really important is the academic performance of athletes *once they are in college* (as underperformance takes its toll).

But I can claim to have made one wiser—if obvious—decision when I concluded that Princeton should stop playing Rutgers in football. The Rutgers program had "big-time" aspirations and was not a good "fit" for Princeton's football program. There was a serious injury to a Princeton player in a Rutgers game that reminds me of Hanna Gray's story of the decision by Robert Hutchins to pull the University of Chicago football program out of the Big Ten. Hutchins said, in effect, that if he didn't step in and do something, the Humane Society would!

I do not believe that there is an easy answer to these large problems, which are rooted in the history of intercollegiate athletics in America, are exacerbated by the fiercely competitive drives of colleges and universities and their alumni, and are complicated enormously by the present-day culture of sports (with young children often encouraged to pursue sports with a daunting intensity). Presidents certainly need to understand these dynamics and should "lean against the wind" in resisting further intensification of intercollegiate sports. Rightly conceived, college sports can be wonderfully beneficial to the individual student and an important part of campus life. We do need to "Reclaim the Game" (the title of the book Sarah Levin and I wrote).

---

[18] See Bowen and Levin, *Reclaiming the Game*, especially 167–69. See also Richard Just's highly perceptive article "Airball" in the March 5, 2010, online edition of the *New Republic*, http://www.tnr.com/book/review/airball. This is another instance in which I learned much more about a problem after leaving the president's office. In the course of the subsequent research just cited, I came across an exceptionally eloquent essay on college sports, highlighting many of these problems thirty years ago, by Yale's president, A. Bartlett Giamatti: "Yale and Athletics," in *The University and the Public Interest* (New York: Athenaeum, 1981), 77–104. Another Yale faculty member, the distinguished economist James Tobin, was also critical of the direction in which athletic recruitment was going in the Ivies even then.

It is a mistake, however, to imagine that there could be a return to a perceived "golden age" when intercollegiate sports were an integral part of a less fragmented campus. There are strong forces favoring ever-greater emphasis on recruitment of ever-more specialized athletes, and there is little any one college or university can do, on its own, to reverse the trend. And it is extremely difficult to get consensus across institutions. Moreover, most busy presidents are understandably reluctant to commit too much of their personal capital to trying to arrest forces that are in some measure beyond their control. I wish I were less pessimistic about prospects for reform—but I do think I am being realistic. The College Sports Project, launched by the Mellon Foundation under the leadership of Eugene Tobin, has proven to be useful in documenting trends and stimulating discussion of what might be done to improve outcomes. Still, the frustrating struggle to achieve even modest reforms within Division III of the National Collegiate Athletics Association (NCAA) is sobering.

As Hanna Gray observed after reading a draft of this book: "There are some difficult problems or situations that you can't fix or do very much about but have to live with, monitor, and at best perhaps hope to see modest amelioration over a long period of time. In any case, one shouldn't pour endless amounts of time and effort where they'll not make much of a difference." I agree entirely with this wise statement of a "lesson learned," which is, I fear, directly relevant to the intrinsic problems with intercollegiate athletics in America today. But one commentator who has been active in reform efforts within the NCAA, Dale Knobel, president of Denison, believes I underestimate what has been accomplished and am too pessimistic about future prospects. I hope he is right.

The emphasis I am placing on the limited capacity of presidents to achieve thoroughgoing reforms should not be interpreted, however, as excusing presidents from failure to oversee athletic programs and to prevent outright cheating and other serious abuses. The disastrous experience of Binghamton University with its men's basketball program is a dramatic illustration of how much damage can be caused by failing to insist on even minimal compliance with NCAA rules, never mind the university's own policies. At Binghamton, all kinds of compromises with academic standards were made—including not just admissions standards, but grading standards after students were enrolled—all in an effort to have a successful Division I program.[19]

Religious Divides: Jewish Students

In sharp contrast to the worrying trends that continue to affect athletic recruitment—which appear to be creating growing athletic/academic divides—many colleges and universities have made substantial progress in reducing religious divides.[20] Institutions of higher education, including those with deep Christian roots, have become far more welcoming to Jewish students and to students of other faiths than they were in days gone by. So much progress has been made that one commentator suggested that this set of issues, especially as it applies to Jewish students, just feels radically different today than it did in earlier years. This is true, but there is always more progress to be made (and more religious groups to be treated with respect, including, of course, Muslims). It would be a mistake, in any case, to believe that the path from there to here was easy or uncomplicated; lessons that remain instructive were learned along the way.

As Morton O. Schapiro, president of Northwestern, says succinctly: "No one wants simply to be tolerated." I agree, and the place of Jewish students on the Princeton campus was an important priority for me since I believed "inclusiveness" meant that all students should feel that Princeton was "their university" and not a place where they were merely

---

[19] Some key basketball players also had serious off-campus legal issues. See Pete Thamel, "Report Faults Binghamton's Leaders in Basketball Scandal," *New York Times*, February 11, 2010 (online edition), for an extensive discussion of the results of the independent investigation ordered by the State University of New York's board of trustees and led by Judith S. Kaye. Binghamton's president, Lois B. DeFleur, is strongly criticized for "taking no corrective action." Fortunately, the SUNY system has a strong leader in its chancellor, Nancy Zimpher, who is highly respected for her tough stance regarding a malfunctioning men's basketball program when she was at the University of Cincinnati.

[20] I focus my discussion here on Jewish students because the historic exclusion of these students from much of campus life (and, for many years, from the university itself) was so egregious. But Catholic students and non-mainline Protestant groups were also often treated as "marginal." The efforts recounted to be more welcoming to Jewish students also helped address the needs of these other religious groups. For an in-depth history of this entire saga, with its roots in the past, see the manuscript under preparation by the former dean of the chapel at Princeton, Frederick Borsch, "Keeping Faith: Religion and Religions at Princeton and Other Universities."

tolerated as "guests." My section of Econ 101 included many able Jewish students, including a number of Orthodox students from Ramaz in New York City.[21] As I came to know these students, it became obvious that a number of them, and their Jewish classmates, felt less fully included in the life of the university than should have been the case. The problem was not so much overt discrimination—though I cannot say that there was none of that—as it was an unstated assumption that Jewish students should simply accommodate themselves to all aspects of university life as they found it. Symbols are important, and there was no overlooking the fact that opening exercises and the baccalaureate service were held in a Christian chapel at the "Christian hour" of 11 a.m. on Sunday. Experience taught us that a thoughtful effort to modify such arrangements could pay large dividends.

Knowing that this was highly sensitive territory, we first involved a diverse faculty group that produced an impressive report on religious life at Princeton, including the place of the university chapel and role of the dean of the chapel. We then constituted a trustee committee, led by John Coburn, a charter trustee who was the Episcopal bishop of Massachusetts. The Jewish members of the faculty committee agreed that official ceremonies should continue to be held in the chapel but not on Sunday mornings; the committee also recommended that these ceremonies should be "truly interfaith in character." In addition, the committee recommended that the next dean of the chapel (the incumbent was retiring) not be seen as a representative of an established Protestant tradition but instead should be charged with encouraging and supporting all religious and spiritual activity on campus. The subsequent trustee report was significantly influenced by the faculty report and adopted all of its main recommendations. As in the case of the earlier consideration of coeducation, the trustees did not press for unanimity, and one member of the trustee committee declined to sign the report—which served, I believe, to give it added credibility.

[21] An aside: In theory, students in Econ 101 were assigned to various sections, including mine, by a random process. But I noticed that I kept getting Ramaz students every year, in spite of the fact that there were not that many of them at the university. When I mentioned this phenomenon to one of these students, he said: "You think this is a coincidence? We figured out the assignment algorithm and chose other classes so that the computer would throw us into this section." So much for randomization.

Immediately following the release of these reports, the university launched a search for a new dean of the chapel, who would be responsible for implementing the recommendations of the committees. We were exceedingly fortunate in recruiting Frederick Borsch, who was a Princeton graduate, an active Episcopalian, and a recognized leader (at Berkeley) in addressing religious concerns on a secular campus. The highly effective efforts of Dean Borsch and the strong support of Trustee Coburn made all the difference in our ability to bring about the needed changes without too much of a struggle with self-styled conservative constituencies that wanted everything to stay as it had always been. The unfortunate experience of William & Mary three decades later in seeking to address a similar problem is a good warning to all presidents that in seeking to achieve change in such a sensitive area, great care has to be taken to proceed deliberately and after full consultation.[22] We are also reminded that new variants of issues of this kind can always present themselves.

Another important part of our "inclusiveness" campaign involved the choice of speakers at the baccalaureate service. For many years, the president of Princeton gave the baccalaureate address, but I thought this unwise since the president also spoke at commencement and Class Day. The seniors and their families deserved more variety than this, and I started inviting others to give the baccalaureate address. My goal from the beginning of this process was to get to a point when I could invite a leading Jewish scholar to speak. But I started out by inviting Trustee Coburn, who had chaired the trustee committee and was, as I have said, a distinguished Episcopalian. I next invited a senior faculty member who was a Protestant clergyman. Next came the president of the Princeton Theological Seminary. I succeeded in persuading Father Hesburgh, president of Notre Dame, to deliver the baccalaureate shortly thereafter.

[22] The president of William & Mary, Gene Nichol, concluded that the Christian trappings of the Wren Chapel were no longer acceptable at what is today meant to be a secular public university. He then acted in what many regarded as a peremptory fashion to remove the cross. There was a huge uproar, and in time the William & Mary board of visitors decided not to renew Nichol's contract, in part (but only in part) as a result of his handling of this matter. Nichol then resigned. For an extensive account of this history, see Bill Geroux, "Former W&M President Nichol Leaving for UNC," *Richmond Times-Dispatch*, March 13, 2008.

In due course, Gerson Cohen, distinguished chancellor of the Jewish Theological Seminary and the father of a graduating senior, agreed to be the speaker. Chancellor Cohen did not disappoint: he gave one of the best baccalaureate addresses in memory, and one of his themes was "that members of one faith can make statements of religious significance to members of other faiths." Cohen went on to remind his audience that "Niebuhr and Maritain can speak to Jews, while Buber and Heschel are studied and appropriated by Christians. . . . The University thus provides a model for the kind of pluralistic society that does not level commitments and differences but refines them through study and calm exchange."[23]

A number of other practical steps were taken, over time, to address dining and residential life issues. First, a kosher kitchen was established; then we organized a few tables in a dining hall where Jewish students could eat kosher meals; finally, a handsome Center for Jewish Life was constructed in a central location. Some thought that the Center for Jewish Life would "ghettoize" the campus, but this did not happen. In fact, the center was extremely useful in providing a place to which non-Jewish students, faculty, and staff could be invited as "guests" of the host Jewish students.

Seeking greater inclusiveness is a never-ending task, but I can say that pursuing this goal was one of the most satisfying things I did in the president's office. The institution was richly rewarded, and I formed a number of enduring friendships through these efforts. The basic principles of inclusiveness are now taken so much for granted that it is hard to recall how challenging it was, only three decades ago, to bring about the necessary changes in university policies and practices.

Residential Life

Ever since Woodrow Wilson's time, issues surrounding residential life have been the subject of lively debate at Princeton. The upper-class eating clubs, which used to be all male and all selective, created innumerable

[23] Gerson Cohen, Baccalaureate Address, Princeton University, June 4, 1978 (copy in Princeton University Archives).

problems for a university seeking to minimize class distinctions, emphasize intellectual values, and treat Jews, Blacks, Hispanics, and Asian Americans (along with all other students) with respect. At the same time, the under-class "Commons" (large dining halls where all first- and second-year students took their meals) was too amorphous and—especially as the student body grew in size—unhelpful in fostering the educational opportunities a residential university should offer.

A number of committees were established to address these issues, and one obvious lesson we learned was that it was much easier to do something about aspects of the problem over which the university had essentially full control (residential life in the freshman and sophomore years) than it was to modify the upper-class club system. The clubs, which provided meals and social life for their members, owned their land and buildings and were supported (often strongly) by their alumni. A successful residential college system was put in place for freshmen and sophomores: students in each of these colleges lived and ate together, and had the benefit of academic and social programs created under the leadership of a faculty master. To be sure, considerable sums of money had to be raised and all sorts of arrangements had to be made so that the academic and residential aspects of college life could be joined together effectively. But, thanks to the generosity of donors and the early leadership of Neil L. Rudenstine, among others, much was accomplished.

Plans were also drawn up to address some of the more troubling aspects of upper-class life, and real progress was made here too (particularly in reducing the near monopoly over social life once exercised by the clubs). But we had to recognize that the university did not have all the levers needed to bring about more fundamental changes.[24]

---

[24] A Committee on Undergraduate Residential Life (CURL) labored mightily on both the under-class and upper-class aspects of residential life at Princeton. It was this committee that recommended the establishment of residential colleges. It also proposed "contracts" with the open-admission upper-class clubs that would have addressed some of their financial problems. But it proved impossible to get enough of the graduate boards of these clubs to agree to this plan—perhaps because they saw the contracts as "the nose of the camel under the tent," that might lead in time to fuller university control. Progress has been made in recent years, however, in organizing shared meal plans between the clubs and the university's residential colleges.

A comparison with the situation at Denison, where I was a trustee, is instructive. Denison had a sorority and fraternity system that created a number of problems, with the fraternities being much more problematic than the sororities in terms of their effects on social life and campus ethos. The president at the time, Michele Myers, was both tough-minded and courageous in leading the board of trustees to prohibit students from living and eating in the fraternities. The fraternities could still exist, but stripping them of their residential character has had an enormous impact. The university had always owned the land under the fraternity houses, and it had owned the buildings as well in three cases. It then purchased four more and secured long-term leases on three others. The buildings were renovated, and all but one now serve as residence halls for men and women. What made this profound change possible were university ownership rights—a telling difference from the situation at Princeton. Some Denison alumni were angry at this decision by the president and trustees, but the positive effects on admission and the "civility" of campus life were so pronounced that opposition was overcome in fairly short order. There is much to be said for not having to rely on facilities outside the control of the university.[25]

I end this chapter by reëmphasizing the importance of a well-structured system of residential life for undergraduates. I understood this need in a general sense from my first encounters with Princeton undergraduates, but it was only considerably later that I came to appreciate the fundamental importance of using the structures of residential life to build community and advance educational values. Princeton today has six fully functioning four-year residential colleges, and I regret that we did not make more progress on this front earlier. Scale matters, and the expansion

[25] Decades earlier, my predecessor as president of the Andrew W. Mellon Foundation, John E. Sawyer, succeeded in addressing a similar problem at Williams College. Many people have told me that President Sawyer's personal leadership was critical to the success of Williams in facing up to a problem with fraternities much sooner than many other colleges and universities. For more about this, see "Statement of the Board of Trustees and Report of the Committee on Review of Fraternity Questions," Williams College, Williamstown, Massachusetts, 1962. See also "End Fraternities, Williams Urged," Special to the *New York Times*, July 2, 1962.

in undergraduate enrollment at Princeton has made it more and more important to create settings in which undergraduate students can live together, in company with faculty masters, directors of studies and student life, resident faculty members, residential college advisors, and graduate students. Similarly, the greater diversity of colleges and universities today calls out for structures that facilitate the kinds of beneficial interactions that we all talk about, but that we don't always achieve.

NINE

Fund-Raising and Alumni Relations

A distinguished neurosurgeon, Wilder Penfield '13, once described Princeton as "an incurable beggar, but stronger than all her patrons." These days, both public and private colleges and universities are indeed "incurable beggars," and a college or university president must play a leading role in raising the funds needed to build and sustain educational excellence. Several commentators (including Derek Bok) have suggested that fund-raising has become much more all-consuming than it used to be. There seems to be almost no time between the end of one campaign and energetic planning for the next, and I know of no real way around this "fact of life." As another president put it: "Feeding the beast is incessant and can really wear you down." Still another commentator suggested that the president today is often "expected to be more 'rainmaker' than intellectual leader."

Recognizing these perceptions, I nonetheless disagree strongly with those who suggest that fund-raising is, at best, a necessary evil. The task is not always as all-consuming as it is sometimes made out to be, and it can be great fun. There is real satisfaction in helping people make better use of their resources than they could ever have made on their own. I was able to encourage the late Don Fisher and his wife, Doris, founders of the Gap and the parents of three Princeton graduates, to pay for a new building for the economics department. At the dedication of the building, as I was thanking the Fishers for their generosity, I was upstaged by Don, who graciously thanked *me* for having given his family the opportunity to do something so rewarding. The Fishers, who were warm personal friends, went on to do a great deal more for Princeton, and it was evident that they derived real pleasure from their gifts—and from the example they set for other parents.

Judith Shapiro, former president of Barnard, had this to say about fund-raising: "When I was on the Charlie Rose show, he asked me whether raising money was disagreeable. I responded that raising money was very agreeable; not raising money was disagreeable. And there is no way I could quantify how much of my time was spent in fundraising, since it was all of a piece: singing the institution's song."[1]

Knowing Your Needs—and Your Donors

An indispensable key to successful fund-raising is to know intimately what the needs of the university are and to be able to articulate those needs in the context of an educational philosophy that resonates with donors. I have never believed in separating the roles of educator and fund-raiser precisely because of this linkage. The goal can never be to raise money for the sake of raising money; it is essential that funds be raised for the right purposes. Having a clear "table of needs" (institutional priorities) from which donors can choose is highly desirable.

It follows that there will be times when turning down a gift is the right course of action. One example comes immediately to mind. Princeton was approached by a major foundation that wanted to make a large gift to establish a program in Korean studies—but a gift not nearly large enough to cover all the associated costs such as creating a proper library collection and supporting graduate students. To the intense annoyance of some colleagues, we turned down the gift. One of my longtime associates, Kevin Guthrie (who did a major study of the New York Historical Society, which was awash in gifts-in-kind that proved to be very difficult to support),

[1] Personal correspondence, February 21, 2010.

likes to offer this advice: "Don't take the Jaguar!" His reference is to a game show in which a participant wins a Jaguar and may be tempted to take the "free" prize without thinking carefully about what it will cost to maintain the car and pay insurance (never mind income tax payments to come).

A second indispensable key to successful fund-raising is to know your donors. One of the most generous donors in Princeton's history is Sir Gordon Y. S. Wu, from Hong Kong. When Gordon agreed to pay for a dining-social complex that was to be the centerpiece of a new residential college at Princeton, he and I reached an understanding that we repeat to each other to this day. My simple formulation: "You thrive, we thrive; if not, not." Gordon more than made good on this understanding when he later made a $100 million pledge. On our side, we assured Gordon that if conditions turned against him in Asia (as they did for a time), we would wait, with him, for conditions to improve. Perseverance is one key to successful fund-raising. Robert Venturi designed the spectacularly successful dining-social center that the university built with Gordon's first gift, and we finally convinced Gordon, after some considerable debate, that it would be appropriate to put his name in Chinese characters over the front door of "Wu Hall." The objective was to say to students from all over the world, as well as to other alumni, that Princeton is not just the product of the generosity of Americans with names like Pyne and Blair, but also of a person named Wu who wanted to give back to a place that was very special to him. It is important when working with donors to be patient and to have a long time horizon—which is one reason, among others, why I have been highly skeptical of the wisdom of tying bonuses for presidents to specific, time-dependent fund-raising results.[2]

More generally, we should never underestimate the willingness of people to give to an institution that they admire. At the time of the discussion of coeducation, there were many comments to the effect that

[2] For a good discussion of this practice, see the story "At Florida State, New President Stands to Profit from University's Fund-Raising Success" in the *Chronicle of Higher Education*, January 14, 2010, http://chronicle.com/article/At-Florida-State-New-Presi/63525/. Raymond D. Cotton, a Washington-based lawyer who works on presidential contracts, warns against turning the president "into a commission-based salesman." A more general worry is that such incentives can encourage fund-raisers to put personal gain over the long-term interest of the donor and the institution. It is also a mistake, in my view, to link presidential pay to gains in *U.S. News* rankings.

women would never match men in their generosity to Princeton. The gift of Meg Whitman, former CEO of eBay, to establish Whitman College speaks for itself.[3] When Princeton seniors, in the spring of 1970, decided to "strike against the Vietnam War" and sent only their class president to march in the reunion P-rade, some alumni described this as "the nadir of Princeton" and opined that these graduates would never support the university. How wrong they were! Just five years later, the Class of 1970 set a record for annual giving by a fifth reunion class. In retrospect, it seems clear that the loyalty of these graduates was only deepened by the experiences they shared in the "Cambodia spring" of 1970.

A related point is that presidents should not be too timid, and should not underestimate the capacity of alumni and other donors to support what may seem to be controversial actions if the case for them is strong. Coeducation is the most vivid Princeton example, but there are also many others. Opposition to change often proves less formidable and less durable than one might have supposed in advance. Preparing the ground carefully, and making good arguments, is of course critically important; but it is also well to recognize that some number of supporters will be inclined to trust the leadership of the institution and respect a willingness to make decisions, even if they entail doing things in a new way. A strong, committed, and effective board of trustees also makes a great difference.

In seeking to raise money, it is of course crucial to hold tight to the values of the institution, as Princeton's experience with Saudi Arabia illustrates so well. Securing funding for the university's major initiative in the life sciences was a top priority, and, thanks to the leadership of a trustee, Gerald Parsky, who had deep knowledge of the Arab world, we made contact with prospective governmental donors in Saudi Arabia and negotiated the outlines of a $5 million gift. From the beginning, the university insisted that any visits associated with the gift be totally free from any hint of discrimination related to gender or religion; otherwise, no gift could be accepted. It came time for a Princeton delegation to travel to

---

[3] A study by Dr. Harvey Rosen and Jonathan Meer determined that "women exhibit significantly both more propensity to make a gift and on average, give gifts of higher amounts." "Determinants of Alumni Giving," Princeton University, 2007.

Riyadh to bring the negotiations to a conclusion, and we stipulated that the Princeton delegation would consist of me (as president), Edward Cox (an eminent biologist), Aaron Lemonick (dean of the faculty and a well-known member of the Jewish community), Marcia Snowden (executive assistant to the president), and Gerald Parsky (the trustee mentioned earlier). There was some initial resistance by the Saudis to the proposed composition of the delegation, but we were firm in stating that we would choose our own members and that there could be no exclusion of Jews or women. The Saudis accepted this understanding and signed a formal agreement underscoring the nondiscriminatory nature of the relationship being built. The ensuing "weekend in Riyadh" (as the student newspaper referred to our trip after we returned) culminated in a most welcome infusion of $5 million into the life sciences.

Not surprisingly, there was great concern in the Jewish community about the gift, with a number of Jewish alumni and others expressing regret that there had been discussions of any kind with Saudi Arabia. We had taken care ahead of time to be sure that the rabbi on the Princeton campus understood exactly what we were doing, including the stipulations that we insisted on. We also enlisted the support of a widely respected member of the Jewish philanthropic community in New York who was a Princeton parent. Thanks to the courage and support of these individuals, among others (including a Jewish alumnus who was the head of the 92nd Street Y), the gift was received without the rancor that it might have engendered. The obvious lesson is the desirability of building support for any such relationship before the deed is done.

At a later date we had an interaction with other representatives of Saudi Arabia that deserves to be mentioned. I was visited by a leading official who indicated that still more support might be forthcoming if we would name the entire academic program for the Saudi king. We were not prepared to do this, and I said to the individual making the request: "Please understand, the University is not for sale—which is precisely why it is so strong and so worth supporting." I am sorry to say that I do not think the message was understood—but it was the right message, and it had to be delivered.

The Robertson Foundation Saga

Of many other fund-raising relationships, I report here on only one—the long-running saga involving the Robertson Foundation that grew out of a magnificent gift to the Woodrow Wilson School of Public and International Affairs. There was a rancorous dispute many years after the gift (and many years after I had left the presidency of Princeton) that led to what some have sought to portray as one of the most important "donor-intent" cases on record.[4] Stripping away innumerable complications, the essential facts are these. In 1961, Marie Robertson, who was married to an alumnus, Charles Robertson, made an initially anonymous gift of $35 million (at a time when the university's total endowment was $80 million) to expand the graduate program of the Woodrow Wilson School for the purpose of augmenting the flow of talented young people into international public service, and especially into positions with the U.S. government. The university established the Robertson Foundation, classified by the Internal Revenue Service as a "supporting organization" of Princeton, to oversee the program established by the Robertsons; the board of this foundation had both members appointed by the university (a majority of the board) and family members, including Charlie Robertson.

The graduate program supported by the Robertson Foundation had its ups and downs, in large part because of the dramatic reversal of attitudes toward government service that resulted from the Vietnam War. A greatly reduced number of students in the Woodrow Wilson School, and at other schools of international affairs, were willing to join the State Department or the Department of Defense. Many Woodrow Wilson School graduates did work in international affairs, but often in positions in non-U.S. organizations such as UNESCO and the World Bank.

There was ongoing debate and discussion about this situation and what could (and could not) be done about it, most of it entirely con-

---

[4] The Robertson family consistently argued that this was a donor-intent case, and it was frequently reported as such in the media. Princeton University, however, vigorously disputed this characterization and believes that the court "was disposed to resolve the core issues within corporate law principles of fiduciary duties and *ultra vires* actions, informed by academic freedom principles." Personal communication from Peter G. McDonough, general counsel of Princeton University, May 5, 2010.

structive, during Charlie Robertson's lifetime. But long after his death (his wife had died earlier), there was litigation. Mr. Robertson's son and other family members argued that the university had violated the stipulations of the gift in spending some of the money on activities such as support for graduate students and faculty in related departments, space renovations, and research programs in international affairs. They also disagreed with the way the university invested the funds provided through the gift. Finally, after years of litigation, with millions of dollars spent on legal fees by both sides, a settlement was reached that redirected a relatively modest share of the assets in the Robertson Foundation (less than 10 percent of the corpus) to other philanthropic purposes chosen by the family and allowed the university to fold the vast bulk of the Robertson Fund into the regular endowment as a restricted gift. The university was then free to move ahead as it thought best—without further involvement from Robertson family members. At the time of the settlement, the corpus of the fund was more than $700 million—after it had been used to pay for the expanded graduate program of the Woodrow Wilson School for forty years—which helps explain what was at stake.[5]

Having been director of the graduate program in the Woodrow Wilson School at the time President Goheen negotiated the gift, and then provost and president—and a member of the board of the Robertson Foundation until I left the presidency—I was deeply involved in this painful and troubling dispute. There was no doubt in my mind that the university had done the right thing in refusing to restrict the activities of the Woodrow Wilson School's graduate program so narrowly that they would have been less successful than they were, and, for that matter, less successful in achieving the original purposes of the gift.

There are several enduring lessons to be drawn from this history. First, when negotiating any gift, be sure that the language is unarguably broad

[5] See the Princeton University Web site for more information about the Robertson case and settlement, specifically, http://www.princeton.edu/robertson/statements/viewstory.xml?storypath=/main/news/archive/S22/81/66C43/index.xml. See also Ben Gose, "Princeton and Robertson Family Settle Titanic Donor-Intent Lawsuit," *Chronicle of Higher Education*, December 10, 2008, http://chronicle.com/article/PrincetonRobertson-Fam/42091/. The "other philanthropic purposes" chosen by the family are to be aligned in perpetuity with the stated purposes of the original Robertson Foundation, albeit as interpreted by Robertson family members.

enough to accommodate unanticipated developments of many kinds—including unpopular wars! (As a commentator with extensive experience in an engineering school reminded me, welding was once an interesting field in what is now materials science—but spare us a professorship in welding.) Second, however tempting it may be to please donors, do not allow the corpus of funds such as this one to be invested separately from the university's endowment. Third, never assume that the children of benefactors will necessarily be as wise or as understanding as the benefactors themselves. Fourth, in using any such gift, follow all proper procedures with exquisite care and keep records that document in fine detail what was done and why—even if this doesn't seem necessary at the time.

I conclude this discussion of fund-raising by suggesting an answer to a frequently asked question: why does a rich university like Princeton always try to raise more money? My short answer: "Progress begets needs." When an institution achieves success in, for example, the life sciences, there are inevitably going to be follow-on needs that have to be met. To provide a specific illustration of this key point: Princeton subsequently—after my time—built the Schultz and Icahn laboratories for the life sciences and is now building a new facility to house neuroscience. Universities are not good at standing pat. They either continue to make progress or fall back. Moreover, any successful college or university will always have far more opportunities to do good in the world than it can possibly fund at any one time. If this is not so, there is a failure of leadership.

Fortunately for Princeton, many donors, and especially those who were undergraduates at the university, have feelings of gratitude, obligation, and confidence in the institution that cause them to continue to be generous to a great university that cannot achieve its full potential without their strong support. Many commentators with experience at other universities have observed that donors often prefer to identify with an institution that is clearly successful, and continuing to make progress, than with an institution that is struggling to maintain its position and perhaps even to survive. Looking ahead, many of us associated with higher education suspect that colleges and universities of all kinds are going to have to work ever harder to raise money from a wider variety of sources. Interested individuals—and organizations—may well want to help and be able to help even as they do not fall into the "traditional" categories of alumnus, parent, or closely connected company or foundation.

Alumni Relations in General

Alumni are of course the main donor base of any private college or university, and are increasingly important for public institutions too. For that reason alone it is important to develop and sustain as positive a set of relationships as possible with them. But this is by no means the only way in which alumni serve their alma mater. In addition to giving money, many alumni are active fund-raisers. As "class agents," they seek annual gifts from classmates, and they are often members of fund-raising committees. They also arrange visits by faculty and administrators to communities across the country and, through local clubs, work to maintain interest in the college or university among alumni, parents, and friends who live in the area. Alumni are also valuable sources of advice, serving on advisory committees of all kinds and as special advisors in key situations (recall the earlier example of George Khoury's pivotal role in the recruitment of leadership for Princeton in the life sciences). "Volunteerism" is a powerful force.[6]

Alumni are valuable advocates, too, sometimes interacting with key governmental officials. To cite just one example, a highly connected alumnus and former trustee of Princeton played an important role in explaining to the White House why President George W. Bush should not send to the Supreme Court a statement opposing all types of race-sensitive admissions. At public universities, alumni regularly play valuable roles in encouraging state governments to support their universities. At essentially all colleges and universities, alumni are active in encouraging promising

[6]Woodrow Wilson's charge to the Princeton Class of 1909 still rings true: "Set out to fulfill obligations, to do what you must and exact of others what they owe you, and all your days alike will end in weariness of spirit.... There is no pleasure to be had from the fulfillment of obligations, from doing what you know you ought to do. Nothing but what you volunteer has the essence of life, the springs of pleasure in it. These are the things you do because you want to do them, the things your spirit has chosen for its satisfaction." *Selected Addresses and Public Papers of Woodrow Wilson*, edited by Albert Bushnell Hart (Honolulu: University Press of the Pacific, 2002), 93.

students to apply for admission and interviewing applicants. After students graduate, alumni often help with job placement and counseling.

There are also rare moments when alumni are called on to undertake quite unusual missions. At the time of Vietnam protests, one disturbed Princeton undergraduate tried to burn down a campus building and ended up in the hands of local police, who were going to send him to the Trenton jail. We learned that if the student's mother would come and pick him up, the judge would release the student in her custody—but we could not reach the mother by phone (line was constantly busy). The vice president for finance had the brilliant idea of searching the alumni directory for people who lived in the same town as the student's mother. He then called an alumnus and said: "I don't have time to explain. Get in your car and go over to the home of 'Mrs. X' and tell her to hang up the phone immediately so that she can take a most important call from Princeton about her son." The alumnus complied with the request and his mission was accomplished (though that was not the end of what turned out to be a complicated saga that I will not describe in greater detail).

Visits by presidents to alumni clubs all over the world are an extremely important means of maintaining contacts, listening to concerns, and communicating the university's message. Anyone who has participated in as many of these gatherings as I have knows that they come in all flavors. One major lesson I learned was the importance of making sure that those in attendance—usually parents as well as alumni—are not too polite. Too much diffidence can obscure legitimate concerns that the president needs to know about. I found it helpful to say quite directly: "There is one rule that we need to honor tonight: no one can leave with a hard question unasked. That is unfair, because if the question is not asked, I have no opportunity to hear it and to respond." Candid exchanges can also serve to stimulate the interest of some alumni who may not have seen any need to be actively engaged with the university. I remember one meeting in Baltimore that became quite testy. After an outspoken alumnus had attacked the university's handling of a sensitive issue in an exceedingly argumentative way, another graduate stood up and said: "After hearing that comment, I now believe that I am actually needed. It is obviously wrong simply to assume that sanity will prevail."

Prickly alumni are often valuable in bringing clarity to issues, and they should be taken seriously and treated with respect. But it is also possible to be too much "on guard" and to expect the worst when in fact there is no reason to do so. Shortly after I was elected president of Princeton, there was a gathering of alumni on campus—at a time when there were many controversial issues. One particularly ferocious-looking alumnus from the Class of 1912 came marching down the hallway toward me, rapping his cane vigorously on the floor. I thought: "Get ready; here comes an assault on the politics of the faculty or on the handling of student protests." I could not have been more wrong. The alumnus in question looked me squarely in the eye and said: "*Young* man [the emphasis was unmistakable], there is just one thing I want you to understand. There is *nothing* you can do to disaffect me!" That comment was a reminder that many of the most faithful alumni are well aware that presidents come and go, but the institution remains—and deserves support whatever mistakes a particular president makes.[7]

Contending with Hostile Groups

I would do a disservice to readers, however (and especially to prospective presidents of colleges and universities), if I glossed over the sometime need to combat alumni attitudes that can be destructive. During my early days in the president's office at Princeton, I had to deal with a group called the Concerned Alumni of Princeton (CAP) that was pursuing what seemed to many a stridently conservative agenda tinged with opposition to co-education, and complaints about alleged coddling of student protestors, aggressive recruiting of minority applicants, the presence of faculty with overtly liberal political views, and so on. The group was well financed and put out a publication that was both tendentious and frequently wrong in its facts. What particularly annoyed my predecessor, Bob Goheen, was the group's inclination to impugn motives.

[7] Another reminder of enduring loyalty was provided by Morton O. Schapiro when he was inaugurated as president of Northwestern. He said how sorry he was that his father-in-law had died recently and could not be present. President Schapiro observed that his father-in-law was a dedicated Harvard graduate of the Class of 1946 who liked to sign some of his letters "Edward Rothman, Harvard '45 (Yale 0)."

Even though the group had been in existence prior to my election, I was not really prepared for this kind of struggle and did not handle the situation very well. At first, I thought that we should just ignore the group and perhaps they would go away. Wrong. Then, after the publication of a story that seriously misrepresented the university's policy on drug use, I went to the other extreme and spent a lot of time and energy rebutting in great detail every claim that CAP made. Wrong again. My overreaction served only to draw attention to the group's activities, to cause them (and others) to think that they were more important than they were, and to encourage them to take more and more extreme positions. Finally, my colleagues and I arrived at a more sensible position. When there were truly damaging and wrongheaded statements made, we corrected the record, but in a low-keyed way. We also declined to be drawn into debates over minor issues. The key to our ultimately successful response to this group was a considered decision not to let them set our agenda. We focused on the issues we thought were really important and said directly that these were the issues we were going to spend serious time on, not issues of lesser consequence that were distractions.

The involvement of others in the debate also helped greatly. The Trustee Committee on Alumni Affairs issued a strongly worded rebuke of CAP in a report that the trustees mailed to all alumni (a report that criticized strongly CAP's claim that they were just "the loyal opposition"). Also, the passage of time, combined with the boredom associated with too much repetition of the same criticisms, contributed to a quiet cessation of activity by the dissident group. Patience, judgment, and "balance" in deciding when and how to respond proved effective.

Times have changed, and email and the Web have made presidents (and everyone else) more accessible to the world at large. They have also reduced the "cycle time" for responding to the crisis du jour. When there is an issue on a campus today, people know about it more or less instantly throughout the world, and everyone feels free to weigh in on the controversy. In this environment, facts and the truth can be distorted quickly. Moreover, as one commentator noted, "it is far easier for people outside the university community to launch cruise missiles from a distance which may do great damage to a campus but have little or no impact on those who have pressed the launch button." It can be easy for a president to get distracted when being bombarded by thousands of messages from outside. It is probably best, in such situations, to focus first on dealing with internal constituencies—and to remind faculty and students that they cannot let themselves be unduly influenced by those with other agendas and little if any stake in the future of the campus community.

Several commentators have asked me to speculate on the reasons why there seems to be so much anti-university sentiment since the 1980s. One recent survey showed that 60 percent of Americans say that colleges care more about the bottom line than about the educational experiences of their students.[8] Economic issues are undoubtedly part of the story. Tuition and fees have regularly outpaced inflation, for reasons that I have tried to explain on numerous occasions.[9] Both families and the media tend to put too much emphasis on "sticker price" and to fail to pay enough attention to the net cost of going to college—which, thanks to financial aid, is often much less than the sticker price for families with need, and also less for other families too because of the widespread use of "discounts" and merit aid. The increased inequality of income in the United States has aggravated this problem, especially for middle-class families. At the same time, other pressures on state budgets—especially the rising costs of health

[8] John Immerwahr and Jean Johnson, with Amber Ott and Jonathan Rochkind, "Squeeze Play 2010: Continued Public Anxiety on Cost, Harsher Judgments on How Colleges Are Run," Report by Public Agenda for the National Center for Public Policy and Higher Education, February 2010, http://www.highereducation.org/reports/squeeze_play_10/index.shtml.

[9] See, for example, my early essay written at the request of Clark Kerr, "The Economics of the Major Private Universities" (a compendium of papers submitted to the Joint Economic Committee, Congress of the United States), in *The Economics and Financing of Higher Education in the United States* (Washington, DC: Government Printing Office, 1969), 399–439; "The Economics of Princeton in the 1970s: Some Worrisome Implications of Trying to Make Do with Less," Annual Report of the President, Princeton University, February 1976; and "Thinking about Tuition" (May 1986), reprinted in *Ever the Teacher*, 527–37. William J. Baumol and I developed the notion of the "cost disease" in our book *Performing Arts: The Economic Dilemma* (Cambridge: MIT Press, 1966; reprinted by Gregg Revivals, 1993), and this tendency for labor-intensive (handicraft) activities to go up in price faster than costs in general rise clearly applies to higher education. I am now involved in a new project designed to see if advances in digital technologies can be used to combat the "cost disease" and increase productivity in higher education.

care—have made it hard for state governments to respond adequately to the legitimate needs of public universities. Given these pressures, colleges and universities must work ever harder both to manage their resources well and to explain their circumstances to the public at large as well as to their own narrower constituencies.

TEN

Life in a President's Office—and When to Leave

One of the most frustrating aspects of life in a president's office is the recurring sense that there is just too much to do—and never enough time to do all that clearly needs to be done. There is no real answer to this problem but two things can help: (1) making sure that you have excellent colleagues who can share the work; and (2) establishing some simple rules as to things that you will not do.

Partners, Colleagues, and Friends

I am very fortunate to have a wife who has always been a real partner. Mary Ellen was (is) superbly well organized, highly knowledgeable about university affairs, calm and patient when I am neither of those things, and unfailingly skillful at arranging and hosting events. She made everyone who came to our house or to official functions feel welcome. She was also a superb listener and alerted me to problems faculty members and their families were having. At the same time, she had a finely tuned sense of how not to interfere with the work of others. When I stepped down as president, the trustees showed their appreciation by naming the main gallery in the art museum in her honor—a well-deserved tribute. Our two children, David and Karen, were also supportive and helpful. Karen enjoyed teasing (and misleading) student reporters who would call the house trying to get information about honorary degree recipients.

I had a team of close colleagues in the president's office who understood what needed to be done and just did it. There is no substitute for having a chief assistant who can both manage people and make decisions. Impeccable judgment is essential, and for sixteen years I had the same chief assistant, Marcia Snowden. In the vernacular, she could "do it all." Everyone who was at all sensible came to understand that if they wanted to get something done, they were well advised to speak first to Marcia. In addition, Marcia and I had a series of exceedingly well-qualified associates who guarded the front door of the office, listened patiently to complaints and suggestions of all kinds, helped with disciplinary matters, and prepared research materials for me. (I preferred to draft my own talks and reports.)[1] It is impossible to exaggerate the importance of such people. Wisdom dictates doing whatever is necessary to recruit the ablest individuals into these positions and then treating them as friends as well as trusted colleagues.

There is also the need to have, just outside the president's office (as it were), other key staff members, including an excellent general counsel. My experience suggests that it is highly desirable to have one's own internal lawyer and not to have to rely exclusively on outside firms, whose attorneys, however talented, can never understand what you are trying to accomplish as fully as an able person who participates in all high-level meetings and is on the scene every day. The internal general counsel will be positioned to take advantage of specialized knowledge that outside firms possess and to manage these relationships. The mindset of the general counsel is very important. It will not do to have someone who always thinks of reasons why you can't do what needs to be done. Rather,

---

[1] I found it very helpful to circulate drafts to colleagues and ask for comments and suggestions. The contributions of these individuals improved my work products considerably. Also, incorporating the good suggestions that I received encouraged those asked to comment to take the review process seriously. There is a broader lesson here: whenever it is possible to take advantage of suggestions of all kinds from faculty and students, as well as administrative colleagues, it is wise to do so. If people learn that they can have an impact in this way, they are more inclined than they would be otherwise to "work through the system."

the shared objective should be to find legitimate ways to move ahead. A good general counsel will advise the president as to the risks involved in taking one action or another, but then will accept the president's judgment as to which risks are and are not worth taking.

There is a close analogy to the role of an outside weather consultant in helping the president decide whether to have commencement inside or outside—a decision that is in fact much more important (certainly to the graduating students and their families) than many outsiders would assume it to be. I had the help of an excellent professional, but I made clear to this person that his job was *not* to decide where commencement was to be held. His job was to tell me the odds that it would rain (and how hard it would rain) at specified hours. It was then my responsibility to take this information and decide what risks to take on behalf of parents and grandparents, as well as the graduates themselves.

Presidents also need real friends—and especially friends on the faculty. Inevitably, mistakes will be made. And there are going to be times when what the president needs most is the capacity to be forgiven for blunders. And my faculty friends were very forgiving! I saw the obverse side of this coin at Denison in the early 1970s. Denison had just recruited a new president with no Denison ties, and when problems arose—as they did on every campus in those days—the new president was left alone to cope as best he could. The unfortunate consequence was that, after some rancorous disputes, he resigned. It would have been so much better if he had had some staunch friends who could have supported him when he needed them the most. There were a few occasions at Princeton when I went to key faculty members and said, in effect, "I don't have time to explain what is happening, but I need you to do X now; trust me, I will explain later." Of course, one cannot go to this well too often, but it is enormously important to be able to go there at least occasionally. There is no substitute for having longtime friends close at hand—to have accumulated "personal capital," as it were, on which you can draw in times of need. As Derek Bok commented, this is one argument in favor of appointing an "insider" as president. In his words: "Good friends will feel able to speak truth to power and to transmit useful gossip or rumblings in the hinterland that a president needs to know."

Deciding What <u>Not</u> to Do as Well as What to Do

It can be tempting to allow others to dictate your agenda, and one cardinal sin, I believe, is to allow yourself to become the slave of your inbox. It is much better, as a wise friend advised me, "to work from your outbox, not your inbox." It is also, I have become convinced, wise to allow a certain amount of "mulching" to occur. Some problems that are not of the highest priority may—occasionally, at least—just go away if time is allowed to pass. This is a hard lesson for compulsive types like me to learn, but learning it can result in an improved allocation of the scarce hours in every day. Hard as it is to know which things can be put in the mulch pile, some can be. It will not do, however, to fail to attend to important tasks simply because they are disagreeable. When I was at the Mellon Foundation, I had a conversation with a newly elected president of a major university who was astonished to discover that he had to deal with problems such as drugs and drinking. I urged him, as diplomatically as I could, to "get real" in understanding his job.

Presidents are inevitably deluged with invitations to do A, B, or C. In thinking about how to respond, I found it helpful to establish ground rules that could be applied in an evenhanded way. One such rule was that I did not give commencement addresses except at Princeton, where by long custom the president was always the commencement speaker. By adhering consistently to this rule, it was possible to turn down invitations without giving undue offense. Another rule was that I did not accept invitations to social events in or around Princeton that did not serve Princeton's interests fairly directly. Learning to say "no" nicely, but firmly, proved to be an important way of protecting time that was needed for other activities. Northwestern's former president, Henry Bienen, reminded me that as president of Princeton, I was "insulated" in a way that he was not in Evanston (Chicago, really)—he had to attend kinds of events that I did not have to attend. Again, setting and context matter.

Most of the "other activities" in which I participated were campus-based or tied to travel for fund-raising or alumni relations. But not all of them. For example, I accepted an invitation in 1974 to join a delegation of college and university presidents from the United States to visit Chinese universities in the immediate aftermath of the Cultural Revolution. That trip was one of the most profound educational opportunities I ever had. Also, I participated in the work of the Association of American Universities (AAU) and the American Council on Education (ACE), in part because of a sense of obligation, but also because these meetings were a valuable opportunity to exchange ideas with colleagues from other universities and be brought up to date on national developments that were important to all of higher education. The regular meetings of the presidents of the Ivy League universities (plus MIT and Stanford) were also valuable opportunities to share ideas and learn from others.

At the same time, these gatherings also taught me how hard it is for collective decision-making to work. Different institutions of higher education naturally have their own objectives, and they are fiercely competitive. Collaboration can work well when there is an unmistakable need for joint action (in support of need-based aid, for example). But in general it is often better to have a trusted third party that is somewhat above the fray—and doesn't have a football team!—to serve as a catalyst. During my time at the Mellon Foundation, colleagues and I did our best to serve this catalytic function, and the creation of JSTOR (a vast digital library of journal literature mentioned earlier that today serves well over 6,000 libraries in more than 150 countries and has more than 35 million pages online) is an example of what can be accomplished using this model. I doubt that any single university, or any collection of universities, could have signed up the publishing partners for JSTOR as quickly as we did, or made innumerable technical and organizational decisions in a timely way.

Let me mention one last decision I made concerning the allocation of time. After careful consideration I accepted a limited number of invitations to serve on outside boards, in both the for-profit and nonprofit sectors. Here, too, I thought I saw opportunities both to learn and to meet people who could be useful to my university in multiple ways. In the for-profit sector, I served on three boards while president (not all at the same time): NCR, Reader's Digest, and Merck. All met in the New York/New Jersey area (a key criterion for economizing on time), and all had lessons to teach on matters of consequence. The Merck board served as an ongoing seminar on research in the life sciences at the very time that Princeton was seeking to build strength in this field. Service on the NCR board brought me in close touch with its chairman and CEO, Charles Exley, a highly intelligent conservative (positioned to the right of Attila the Hun, as he liked to say) whose comments improved many of the reports I drafted on controversial subjects such as affirmative action. Reader's Digest, which was owned by philanthropic interests, taught lessons about how difficult it can be to escape old ways of thinking. The American Express board, which I joined after leaving Princeton, taught me lasting lessons about how to manage transitions in leadership.

Apart from the educational value of these associations, I felt that there was a symbolic point to be made: How could the university expect leaders of such organizations to serve on its board and work hard on its behalf if the university president was unwilling himself to make at least a modest contribution to their governance? There are, of course, also downsides to serving on outside boards, starting with the time they consume. And it is obviously important to avoid serving on boards that will prove embarrassing—either because of what the company does or because of its leadership.

A most important lesson I learned about time management is the need to save some serious time for activities that *you* want to do. As mentioned earlier, I taught a section of beginning economics every year that I was president (with the single exception of a year when I had a partial leave of absence to draft a campaign prospectus). I enjoyed these contacts with students immensely, and I have maintained to this day friendships with several of them, including Robert Rawson, a distinguished attorney who became chairman of the Executive Committee of Princeton's board after I left the university. It was also stimulating to introduce students of the caliber of Tim Scanlon (now a distinguished professor of philosophy at Harvard) and Eric Lander (now founding director of the Broad Institute of MIT and Harvard) to the wonders of general equilibrium theory—which both more or less deduced on their own. I fear that I drove both of these incredibly bright people from economics, but that may be just as well; they have certainly thrived in their chosen fields.

There is much to be said for seeing students in their natural (classroom) habitat. Students in my Econ 101 classes were invaluable sources of information as to what was working and what needed fixing at the university, and talking with them was a good corrective to obligatory meetings with many politically engaged student leaders who visited me in my office.[2] The president also needs to spend time with the student press, and I can report that in general I enjoyed my exchanges with the reporters and editors who covered my office. I did my best to be entirely straightforward with them, and in the main they reciprocated by trying hard to get stories right. That was essential, because the student newspaper was the most important vehicle for communicating with the campus community, and its stories often became the basis for commentary by the national press. There were, to be sure, exceptions to "good behavior," and one of my predecessors, Harold Dodds, became so annoyed by articles that at one juncture his doctor would not allow him to look at the *Daily Princetonian* until his health improved! I should add that working with student reporters always seemed to me to be another form of teaching, and I was rewarded by opportunities to get to know some truly outstanding undergraduates who ran the paper.

When asked why I spent so much time teaching Econ 101, I had a ready answer: "For the most selfish reason. I enjoy it." There is, however, a broader point to underscore. If the president allows his or her schedule to consist primarily of endless meetings that the president simply has to attend, real weariness of spirit can set in. For some people, setting aside regular time to visit museums serves the same purpose that teaching— and athletics—served for me. (I was a fiercely competitive squash and tennis player, and I have often said that athletics was, for me, a more or less harmless outlet for aggression.) Others will want to travel to new places with their families and friends. Columbia's president, Lee Bollinger, is known for his "5K Fun Runs" and for reserving time for daily runs of his own—as well as time for backpacking and camping in remote places. The specific activity matters much less than the benefit that can come when the president has some opportunity to recharge batteries by doing what he or she really enjoys most. As I said to one president who was, I thought, trying to do too much: "You must be at least a little selfish in managing

[2] To be fair, there were also some exceptional leaders of student organizations who made major contributions to Princeton. One student I mentioned earlier, Jerome Davis '71, was the leader of both the undergraduate student government and the Association of Black Collegians at a time when strong leadership of those organizations made a tremendous difference. Jerome is today among our family's closest friends.

your time, or you will not be able to function well when doing presidential things; you will not be useful to anyone."

I also learned early in my time as president that it was valuable to have a place away from the campus where I could go to think and write free of the constant interruptions that were hard to limit when on the campus. With the lively encouragement of the university's financial vice president, my wife and I bought property in Avalon, New Jersey, near Cape May, which was far enough away to be "away" but close enough (a two-hour drive through the Pine Barrens) that I could go back and forth on weekends and also get back quickly should an emergency arise.

A final point about life in the president's office: I learned that it is important to say clearly and forcefully what you believe on important university-related matters. It is unwise to equivocate too much or shy away from controversy. The president must speak up even if the result is that some people are annoyed. Not long ago I came across a fortune cookie with this message: "To avoid criticism, do nothing, say nothing, be nothing." A related point is that accountability means giving reasons for policies you have adopted and decisions you have made. Inevitably, there will be criticism from all sides, but that just needs to be understood and accepted. In discussing Russian writers who understood how hard it was to seize on absolutes and how easy it was to offend those on both extremes, Isaiah Berlin wrote: "The middle ground is a notoriously exposed, dangerous, and ungrateful position."[3] It is. Yet, as Berlin understood so well, the complexities of important issues often force a thoughtful person to acknowledge that there are many sides to most questions of moment.

On Leaving

There is no formula for determining how long it makes sense to serve as president of a college or university. Much depends on an individual's age and health, on successes and satisfactions as well as frustrations, on fundraising calendars, and of course on relationships with faculty and trustees.

[3] Isaiah Berlin, "Fathers and Children," in *Russian Thinkers* (London: Penguin Books, 1978), 297.

And, needless to say, it isn't always the president who decides when he or she should leave!

A wise friend of mine, David Culver (a Canadian business executive with long ties to McGill University), offers this advice for living a good life: set reasonable near-term goals; take satisfaction from small achievements; and "always have an alternative." The last part of this injunction is especially important, I think, since you never want to be in the position of feeling that you have to hang on to your job no matter what. Being trapped in a position can force unwise compromises and, in general, lead to unhappiness. Knowing that you "always have an alternative" frees a person to do what seems to be the right thing, whatever the consequences.

In general, it is desirable to stay in a presidency long enough to have a real impact. Planning to stay a minimum of eight to ten years is, I think, a good target. In my own case, some of the most important things I was able to accomplish came near the end of a tenure of nearly sixteen years. It takes time to learn the lay of the land—where the bodies are buried. Too short a term is often disruptive for the institution, since search processes can be tedious, the outcome uncertain, and transitions sometimes more complicated than one would like them to be. But situations and personalities differ, and I certainly respect the decision of Erskine Bowles to retire as president of the University of North Carolina after five exceedingly active years as the leader of that great university system. In announcing his retirement, President Bowles declared: "From Day One I have been very candid in saying publicly that my approach and my style of leadership can exact a heavy toll on the people who work with me, and that as a result, five years would be about all of Erskine Bowles anyone could stand."[4] Accurate or not as that statement may be (and I am skeptical that Bowles is in fact that hard on those who work with him), once a president has reached the decision that he made, all that his colleagues

[4]Statement of President Erskine B. Bowles to his colleagues announcing his plans to retire as president (February 12, 2010). It is interesting to note the similarity between President Bowles's thinking and the decision by another highly activist leader, Mamphela Ramphele, to step down as vice-chancellor of UCT after a relatively short time in office. (See discussion at the end of chapter 6.)

can or should do is thank him for his service and allow him to move on without feelings of guilt.

It is, of course, also possible to stay too long—almost certainly a more common error. Tempting as it can be to want to stay until all is in order, that may be an unachievable goal. In an institution as complex as a college or university, there is rarely if ever a time when "all is in order."

I am a firm believer in the adage "Leave when there is at least some semblance of a band playing." It is a profound mistake to overstay a welcome. In an entirely different context (the forced departure of a CEO of a for-profit firm after prolonged debate within the company about his tenure), a friend of the CEO reflected on the embarrassing consequences for the individual of his failure to understand sooner that he had to go: "Sadly, it's now too late for [his friend] to graduate." One internal signal of when the time has come to contemplate moving on is when you begin to bore yourself by, for example, retelling the same stories too often. When Oprah Winfrey announced that she was leaving her daytime TV show, the *New York Times* titled its story "The Fine Art of Quitting While She's Ahead."[5] It is gratifying to feel, as I did, that I was still enjoying my work as president enormously when I decided that it was time to make way for someone else who would bring a freshness to the position ("new stories"). There is a proper rhythm in life for both institutions and individuals, and that rhythm deserves to be respected.

One leader of a higher education search firm reports having had two assignments that involved coping with the debilitating legacies of presidents who simply "ran out of gas." In his words, "they stopped going the extra mile to be personally engaged in campus life. . . . Perhaps most problematically, their circle of advisers became narrower and narrower." Key constituencies lost confidence in leaders they had once respected, with dispiriting consequences for all concerned.[6] Presidents need honest, forthright friends who will help them see when it is time to move on. Carefully managed reviews of presidential performance can also be valuable, and I am pleased that such regular reviews are now commonplace

---

[5] Alessandra Stanley, *New York Times*, November 20, 2009.

[6] Dennis M. Barden, "It's Hard to Say Goodbye," *Chronicle of Higher Education*, April 25, 2010, http://chronicle.com/article/Its-Hard-to-Say-Goodbye-E/65236/.

in higher education, as they were not when I was president of Princeton. Such reviews can also be helpful in assisting presidents to learn how they can be more effective while they are still in office.

My final piece of advice can be stated succinctly: When you leave, leave! As I have said on various occasions following my departure from Princeton, "One president at a time is enough—maybe more than enough!"[7] Genuinely fresh thinking, including a reëxamination of established policies and procedures, is healthy, and much easier to achieve in the absence of the person who was responsible for putting in place many of the policies and procedures in question. For-profit organizations have come rather belatedly to recognize that it is almost always a mistake to keep a retired CEO on the board. In the college/university world, that would be unlikely in any case, but finding other ways of making sure that there is some real distance between the retired president and the institution is in everyone's interest—and certainly in the interest of the institution itself. To be sure, new presidents may seek advice from their predecessors, but it should be entirely up to the new president to decide when—if at all—such advice is needed. The outgoing president may be helpful, however, in assuring friends and former colleagues that they should expect—and welcome—a new style of leadership.

"One should never look for birds of this year in the nests of yesteryear." That is the advice that Cervantes had Don Quixote offer on his deathbed.[8] I have had on my desk for many years an alabaster calendar with an equally wise injunction attributed to the naturalist John Burroughs: "New times always, old time we cannot keep."

[7] Michael McPherson recalled that as he was preparing to leave the president's office at Macalester College, he was told about the double-decker buses in London—the ones where you could just step aboard and hold on to a pole. Supposedly there was a sign on the back, reminding passengers: "When you step off, please let go." In this personal correspondence to me, Mike added: "I've always thought that was the right advice."

[8] Miguel de Cervantes Saavedra, *Don Quixote of La Mancha*, edited and translated by Walter Starkie (New York: Signet, 1979), 1048.

ELEVEN

Epilogue: Why Colleges and Universities Matter So Much

A final lesson I have learned—and learned again and again—is what a privilege it has been to be closely associated with colleges and universities all of my adult life. These institutions are tremendously important to the country for the most mundane reason: they are powerful engines of economic opportunity. They are vital to maintaining our competitive position in an increasingly knowledge-dependent world economy. They are important too to the social fabric of the country: they are engines of social mobility as well as economic progress.

Compelling as they are, these basic propositions are not what I want to emphasize in concluding this book. In addition to their indispensable economic, social, and political contributions, these enduring institutions have so much else to teach us. It is our passion for them and for the values they represent that drives us forward. Their often-long histories exemplify the continuing power of certain habits of mind and heart, including openness to new ideas and new friendships, respect for both evidence and the beauty of language, appreciation of "difference," and an ever-deeper awareness of the pure joy of learning.

To underscore the last point, I offer two testimonials, one from an undergraduate and one from a distinguished scholar.

144

- An undergraduate, speaking at an alumni gathering in 1980, said that one of Princeton's most lasting gifts to its students is a sense of joy that "springs from the beauty of the campus, from the whimsy of countless black and orange tigers, both two-legged and four-legged, and above all, from our unceasing discoveries of the promise within Princeton and within ourselves."[1]

- One of my greatest teachers, Professor Jacob Viner, paid this tribute to scholarship at a Brown University graduate school commencement in 1950: "All that I plead on behalf of scholarship is that, once the taste for it has been acquired, it gives a sense of largeness even to one's small quests, and a sense of fullness even to the small answers to problems large or small which it yields, a sense which can never in any other way be attained, for which no other source of human gratification can, to the addict, be a satisfying substitute, which gains instead of loses in quality and quantity and pleasure-yielding capacity by being shared with others—and which, unlike golf, improves with age."[2]

The issues that confront one university, and one university president, at one point in time, often have strong echoes at other institutions and in other times. To be sure, some problems, and some opportunities, are unique to particular institutions. But many of the most important questions that present themselves are more common than not. Commitments to freedom of expression and to the education of a diverse as well as talented set of students clearly fall into this category. In thinking about such pervasive aspects of our mission, and how to sustain them, I am struck by the importance of institutional memory and how often it is lacking. As important as it is to seek new perspectives, it is just as important to understand how structures and choices have evolved over time.

[1] Ronald D. Lee, Pyne Prize Acceptance Speech, February 23, 1980; Office of the President Records: William G. Bowen, Box 358, Folder 12; University Archives, Department of Rare Books and Special Collections, Princeton University.

[2] Jacob Viner, "A Modest Proposal for Some Stress on Scholarship in Graduate Training," Address before the Graduate Convocation, Brown University, June 3, 1950. Brown University Papers XXIV, 1950.

We are well advised, I think, to celebrate, not to bemoan, what one of my student friends liked to refer to as "the heavy weight of the past."

At their best, academic institutions help students and faculty members see education as a "long journey," enormously consequential in its own right. "Hope the voyage is a long one, / full of adventure, full of discovery," Cavafy writes in his evocative poem "Ithaka" (the island home of Odysseus, to which he returned after the Trojan War and many years of wandering). Cavafy continues: "May there be many a summer morning when / with what pleasure, what joy, / you come into harbors seen for the first time; / . . . But do not hurry the journey at all. / Better if it lasts for years, / so you are old by the time you reach the island, / wealthy with all you have gained on the way."[3]

Colleges and universities are special in many respects. They have distinctive purposes that bridge chasms. As the historian Richard Hofstadter put it in a memorable commencement address at Columbia, the university is poised delicately between "its position in the external world, with all its corruption and evils and cruelties, and the splendid world of our imagination."[4] In many college and university communities, there is a welcome blurring of the lines between work and play and between the professional and personal sides of one's life. This is, I think, why so many of us have been able to form rich friendships in the university "workplace." In addition, these institutions give those associated with them the opportunity to acquire an enhanced sense of service—of obligations to others. We are reminded regularly that, as a wise trustee friend (Harold H. Helm) was fond of saying, "It's healthy to spend some time with other people's problems."

Perhaps above all, colleges and universities are symbols of continuity. They are long-term creators of knowledge and understanding, with each generation benefiting from the work of its predecessors as it, in turn, presents new challenges and opportunities to the next. Robert K. Merton's book *OTSOG* (On the Shoulders of Giants) captures beautifully this notion

---

[3] *C. P. Cavafy: Collected Poems,* revised edition, translated by Edmund Keeley and Philip Sherrard, edited by George Savidis (Princeton: Princeton University Press, 1992), 36–37.

[4] Hofstadter, "Columbia University Commencement Address for the 214th Academic Year," 384.

of building on the achievements of others.[5] Through their settings, their traditions, and even their commencement regalia, they create a sense of order, a sense of being part of an endless historical progression—and at a time when there is so little cohesion and "reconciling ceremony" in the world around us. Failings and shortcomings notwithstanding, we do well to protect and strengthen these venerable institutions that have nurtured and inspired so many over the centuries.

[5] Robert K. Merton, *On the Shoulders of Giants* (Chicago: University of Chicago Press, 1965). The phrase "On the Shoulders of Giants" is often associated with Sir Isaac Newton's response to Robert Hooke in a seventeenth-century debate over the priority of discovery of properties of light and color. Newton wrote: "You defer too much to my ability for searching into this subject. What Descartes did was a good step. You have added much. . . . If I have seen further, it is by standing on the shoulders of giants."

ACKNOWLEDGMENTS

One large theme of this book is the importance of collaborations—between trustees and resident campus communities; among administrators across campuses; among administrators, faculty, staff, students, and alumni within particular institutions; and among the leaders of colleges and universities more generally.

It is fitting, then, that in writing *Lessons Learned* I have benefited greatly from the comments of an unusually large number of highly knowledgeable colleagues and friends. These comments were so helpful that I have inserted many of them in the text, sometimes with the commentator's name, sometimes not, depending on what seemed appropriate. Thus, the text is itself a kind of collaboration. With renewed thanks to each and every one, I list here these commentators.

Lawrence S. Bacow, president of Tufts University and former chancellor of MIT

Paul Benacerraf, former provost and professor of philosophy, Princeton University

Henry S. Bienen, former president of Northwestern University

Derek Bok, former president of Harvard University

Frederick Borsch, former dean of the chapel at Princeton University

Mary Ellen Bowen, former president of the Auxiliary to the Isabella McCosh Infirmary at Princeton; wife of a university president

D. Ronald Daniel, former treasurer of Harvard University and member of the Corporation; trustee of Brandeis University and former trustee of Wesleyan University; former managing director of McKinsey & Company

Jerome Davis, secretary of Columbia University

Robert Durkee, secretary of Princeton University

Christopher L. Eisgruber, provost of Princeton University

Hanna Holburn Gray, former president of the University of Chicago and of Yale University

Kevin Guthrie, founding president of JSTOR and president of Ithaka Harbors

Amy Gutmann, president of the University of Pennsylvania

Sheldon Hackney, former president of the University of Pennsylvania and of Tulane University; former chairman of the National Endowment for the Humanities

Nicholas deB. Katzenbach, former attorney general and undersecretary of state of the United States; former trustee of Princeton University

John C. Kenefick, former chairman of the Executive Committee of the Princeton University Board of Trustees; retired chairman and CEO of the Union Pacific Railroad

Nannerl O. Keohane, former president of Duke University and of Wellesley College

Dale T. Knobel, president of Denison University

Richard Lyman, former president of Stanford University

Nancy Weiss Malkiel, dean of the college, Princeton University

Mary Patterson McPherson, president of the American Philosophical Society; former president of Bryn Mawr College

Michael S. McPherson, president of the Spencer Foundation and former president of Macalester College

Michele Tolela Myers, former president of Sarah Lawrence College and of Denison University

Stephen Oxman, chairman of the Executive Committee of the Princeton University Board of Trustees; advisory director of Morgan Stanley

Nancy B. Peretsman, member of the Princeton University Board of Trustees; managing director of Allen & Company

W. Taylor Reveley III, president of the College of William & Mary

Frank H. T. Rhodes, former president of Cornell University

Neil L. Rudenstine, chairman of ARTstor; former president of Harvard University; former provost of Princeton University

Morton O. Schapiro, president of Northwestern University; former president of Williams College

Judith Shapiro, former president of Barnard College

James Shulman, president of ARTstor

Marcia Snowden, former executive assistant to the president, Princeton University

T. Dennis Sullivan, president and CEO of the Church Pension Group, Episcopal Church of America; former president of the Princeton University Investment Company (Princo); former financial vice president of the Andrew W. Mellon Foundation

Eugene M. Tobin, program officer of the Andrew W. Mellon Foundation; former president of Hamilton College

Sarah E. Turner, professor of education and economics, University of Virginia

Daniel H. Weiss, president of Lafayette College

Lynn Wendell, educational consultant; trustee and officer of the San Francisco Conservancy; former board chair of San Francisco University High School

Peter C. Wendell, general partner in Sierra Ventures; charter trustee and board officer at Princeton University; director of Merck (NYSE-MRK) and chairman of its audit committee; faculty member of Stanford Business School; former chairman of the board of the Princeton University Investment Company (Princo)

The book is dedicated to four lifelong friends who have taught me many of the lessons recounted here: **Paul Benacerraf**, **Mary Ellen Bowen**, and **Neil L. Rudenstine**, whose names appear on the list of commentators; and the late **Stanley Kelley Jr.**, professor of politics at Princeton. Stan Kelley joined the Princeton faculty at almost exactly the same time that I did (in the late 1950s), and he and I were friends and colleagues for over half a century. His singular role in shaping the governance of Princeton and, indirectly, the governance of many other institutions of higher education, is detailed in chapter 2. Had Professor Kelley lived longer, and been able to comment on the manuscript, my work product would surely have been improved greatly.

I will also always be indebted to the late **Robert F. Goheen**, my predecessor as president of Princeton and one of my greatest teachers. The Princeton trustees with whom I worked were also unfailing sources of encouragement, good advice, and criticism. I was so fortunate to watch in action four exceedingly able chairs of the Executive Committee of the Princeton University Board of Trustees: the late **Harold H. Helm**, the late **R. Manning Brown Jr.**, **John C. Kenefick**, and **James Henderson**. Special mention should also be made of two other longtime trustees with whom I had memorable—and highly instructive—debates, over tuition policy and countless other issues: **W. Michael Blumenthal** and **Paul Volcker**. I am proud to say that both of these sage contrarians have remained good friends—and cheerful critics!—to this day.

Among the many others who contributed to *Lessons Learned*, I must single out

- **Johanna Brownell**, my chief assistant in New York, who has been a key partner in this project from the beginning. Johanna did a great deal of research unearthing materials. She has gone over countless drafts, caught innumerable errors, made good suggestions, and put the final manuscript in what I hope is presentable form.

- **Susanne Pichler**, librarian of the Andrew W. Mellon Foundation, who has been an invaluable contributor to this book as to many others. Susanne can always find the most obscure references, and she has been an unfailing source of ideas for materials to cite that would have escaped me.

- **Daniel J. Linke**, archivist of Princeton University, who found many documents that were needed for the book—and always with good humor and no complaints.

- **Ann Halliday**, the exceedingly able assistant secretary of Princeton University, who was always our first port of call when we needed help of any kind from the university.

- **Peter J. Dougherty**, director of the Princeton University Press, who was far more than just a superb editor. Peter provided framing ideas and challenging questions, along with encouragement, at every step along the way.

It remains only to say that I alone am responsible for whatever errors I have failed to catch.

William G. Bowen
April 2010

REFERENCES

Avery, Christopher, Andrew Fairbanks, and Richard Zeckhauser. *The Early Admissions Game: Joining the Elite*. Cambridge: President and Fellows of Harvard College, 2003.

Bain and Company. "Achieving Operational Excellence at University of California, Berkeley, Final Diagnostic Report—Complete Version." April 2010. http://berkeley.edu/oe/phase1/phase1-full.pdf.

Barden, Dennis M. "It's Hard to Say Goodbye." *Chronicle of Higher Education*, April 25, 2010. http://chronicle.com/article/Its-Hard-to-Say-Goodbye-E/65236/.

Berger, Joseph. "An Undocumented Princetonian." *New York Times Magazine*, January 3, 2010.

Berlin, Isaiah. *Russian Thinkers*. London: Penguin Books, 1978.

The Best of PAW. Princeton: Princeton Alumni Weekly, 2000.

Bogle, John C. *Enough: True Measures of Money, Business and Life*. Hoboken: John Wiley and Sons, 2009.

Borsch, Frederick. "Keeping Faith: Religion and Religions at Princeton and Other Universities." Manuscript under preparation.

Bowen, William G. "Admissions and the Relevance of Race." *Princeton Alumni Weekly*, September 26, 1977.

———. *The Board Book*. New York: W. W. Norton, 2008.

———. "The Economics of the Major Private Universities." In *The Economics and Financing of Higher Education in the United States*, 399–439. Washington, DC: Government Printing Office, 1969.

———. "The Economics of Princeton in the 1970s: Some Worrisome Implications of Trying to Make Do with Less." Annual Report of the President, Princeton University, February 1976.

———. *Ever the Teacher*. Princeton: Princeton University Press, 1988.

———. "The Two Faces of Wealth." Remarks at the Induction of Morton O. Schapiro as 16th President of Williams College, October 21, 2000.

———. "University Salaries: Faculty Differentials." *Economica*, new series, 30, no. 120 (1963): 341–59.

Bowen, William G., with W. J. Baumol. *Performing Arts: The Economic Dilemma*. Cambridge: MIT Press, 1966. Reprinted by Gregg Revivals, 1993.

Bowen, William G., and Derek Bok. *The Shape of the River: Long-Term Consequences of Considering Race in College and University Admissions*. Princeton: Princeton University Press, 1998.

Bowen, William G., and Julius L. Chambers. "The Duke Administration's Response to Lacrosse Allegations." http://www.dukenews.duke.edu/mmedia/pdf/Bowen-ChambersReportFinal05-04-06.pdf.

Bowen, William G., Matthew M. Chingos, and Michael S. McPherson. *Crossing the Finish Line: Completing College at America's Public Universities*. Princeton: Princeton University Press, 2009.

Bowen, William G., Martin A. Kurzweil, and Eugene M. Tobin. *Equity and Excellence in American Higher Education*. Charlottesville: University of Virginia Press, 2005.

Bowen, William G., and Sarah A. Levin. *Reclaiming the Game*. Princeton: Princeton University Press, 2003.

Bowen, William G., and Neil L. Rudenstine. *In Pursuit of the PhD*. Princeton: Princeton University Press, 1992.

Cavafy, C. P. *Collected Poems*. Revised edition. Translated by Edmund Keeley and Philip Sherrard. Edited by George Savidis. Princeton: Princeton University Press, 1992.

Cervantes Saavedra, Miguel de. *Don Quixote of La Mancha*. Edited and translated by Walter Starkie. New York: Signet, 1979.

Cohen, Gerson. Baccalaureate Address, Princeton University, June 4, 1978. Princeton University Archives.

Cole, Jonathan. *The Great American University*. New York: Public Affairs, 2010.

Davis, Jerome. "A New Day for Black and White." *Princeton Alumni Weekly*, October 21, 1969.

——. "Statement Written on Behalf of ABC (Association of Black Collegians) for the Princeton University Yearbook *Bric*," 1970.

Dillon, Sam. "New Jersey College Is Beset by Accusations." *New York Times*, December 22, 2009.

——. "New Jersey Has Settled with a College It Sued." *New York Times*, January 16, 2010.

"End Fraternities, Williams Urged." Special to the *New York Times*, July 2, 1962.

Fields, Carl. "The Black Arrival at Princeton." *Princeton Alumni Weekly*, April 18 and 25, 1977. Reprinted in *The Best of the PAW*, 327–35.

Forster, E. M. *Pharos and Pharillon*. New York: Alfred A. Knopf, 1961.

Fox, John D. "The Hiss Hassle Revisited." *Princeton Alumni Weekly*, May 3, 1976. Reprinted in *The Best of PAW*, 251–61.

Friend, Tad. "Letter from California: Protest Studies." *New Yorker*, January 4, 2010.

Geroux, Bill. "Former W&M President Nichol Leaving for UNC." *Richmond Times-Dispatch*, March 13, 2008.

Giamatti, A. Bartlett. *The University and the Public Interest*. New York: Athenaeum, 1981.

Gose, Ben. "Princeton and Robertson Family Settle Titanic Donor-Intent Lawsuit." *Chronicle of Higher Education*, December 10, 2008. http://chronicle.com/article/PrincetonRobertson-Fam/42091/.

Gurin, Patricia, with Eric L. Dey, Gerald Gurin, and Sylvia Hurtado. "The Educational Value of Diversity." http://141.211.86.200/pdf/0472113070-ch3.pdf.

Gutmann, Dr. Amy. Inaugural Address, University of Pennsylvania, October 15, 2004. https://secure.www.upenn.edu/secretary/inauguration/speech.html.

Hoekma, David. *Campus Rules and Moral Community*. Boston: Rowman and Littlefield, 1994.

Hofstadter, Richard. "Columbia University Commencement Address for the 214th Academic Year." In *American Higher Education Transformed 1940–2005: Documenting the National Discourse*, edited by Wilson Smith and Thomas Bender, 383–86. Baltimore: Johns Hopkins University Press, 2008.

Hoxby, Caroline M. "The Changing Selectivity of American Colleges." Working Paper 15446, NBER Working Paper Series October 2009. http://www.nber.org/papers/w15446.

Immerwahr, John, and Jean Johnson, with Amber Ott and Jonathan Rochkind. "Squeeze Play 2010: Continued Public Anxiety on Cost, Harsher Judgments on How Colleges Are Run." Report by Public Agenda for the National Center for Public Policy and Higher Education, February 2010. http://www.highereducation.org/reports/squeeze_play_10/index.shtml.

Jaschik, Scott. "Race and Merit at MIT." *Inside Higher Ed*, January 15, 2010. www.insidehighered.com/news/2010/01/15/mit.

Jones, Landon Y. "The Hickel Heckling." *Princeton Alumni Weekly*, May 26, 1970. Reprinted in *The Best of PAW*, 336–344.

Just, Richard. "Airball." *New Republic*, March 5, 2010. http://www.tnr.com/book/review/airball.

Karabel, Jerome. *The Chosen: The Hidden History of Admission and Exclusion at Harvard, Yale, and Princeton*. Boston: Houghton Mifflin, 2005.

Kelley, Stanley, Jr. "The Governing of Princeton University: Final Report of the Special Committee on the Structure of the University." Princeton University, April 1970. http://diglib.princeton.edu/ead/getEad?id=ark:/88435/w37636770.

Kennedy, Donald. *Academic Duty*. Cambridge: Harvard University Press, 1997.

Koblik, Steven, and Steven R. Graubard, eds. *Distinctively American: The Residential Liberal Arts Colleges*. New Brunswick, NJ: Transaction Publishers, 2000.

Lederman, Doug. "Tangled Web at Wesleyan." *Inside Higher Ed*, January 6, 2010. http://www.insidehighered.com/news/2010/01/06/wesleyan.

Lee, Ronald D. Pyne Prize Acceptance Speech, February 23, 1980. Office of the President Records: William G. Bowen, Box 358, Folder 12; University Archives, Department of Rare Books and Special Collections, Princeton University.

Lewis, Bernard. *The Jews of Islam*. Princeton: Princeton University Press, 1984.

Lyall, Sarah. "Unclear Outcome at Polls Adds Urgency to Issue of Electoral Overhaul in Britain." *New York Times*, May 8, 2010.

Lyman, Richard W. *Stanford in Turmoil*: Stanford: Stanford University Press, 2009.

Masterson, Kathryn. "At Florida State, New President Stands to Profit from University's Fund-Raising Success." *Chronicle of Higher*

Education, January 14, 2010. http://chronicle.com/article/
At-Florida-State-New-Presi/63525/.

McCray, Melvin, and Calvin Norman. *Looking Back: Reflections of Black
Princeton Alumni.* Video. 1997.

Merton, Robert K. *On the Shoulders of Giants.* Chicago: University of Chicago
Press, 1965.

Posner, Richard. "Larry Summers and Women Scientists—Posner." http://
www.becker-posner-blog.com/archives/2005/01/.

"Report on the Initiative for Faculty Race and Diversity." Massachusetts Institute of Technology, January 14, 2010.

Reveley, W. Taylor, III. "No Discrimination at W&M." http://www.wm.edu/
news/pressreleases/2010/no-discrimination-at-wm.php.

Rosen, Dr. Harvey, and Jonathan Meer. "Determinants of Alumni Giving."
Princeton University, 2007.

Rosovsky, Henry. *The University: An Owner's Manual.* New York: W. W. Norton,
1991.

Saunders, Stuart. *Vice-Chancellor on a Tightrope: A Personal Account of
Climactic Years in South Africa.* Cape Town: David Philip Publishers,
2000.

Schrecker, Ellen. *No Ivory Tower: McCarthyism and the Universities.* New York:
Oxford University Press, 1986.

Shulman, James L., and William G. Bowen. *The Game of Life: College Sports
and Educational Values.* Princeton: Princeton University Press, 2001.

Stanley, Alessandra. "The Fine Art of Quitting While She's Ahead." *New York
Times,* November 20, 2009.

"Statement of the Board of Trustees and Report of the Committee on Review
of Fraternity Questions." Williams College, Williamstown, Massachusetts, 1962.

Steele, Claude. *Whistling Vivaldi and Other Clues to How Stereotypes Affect Us.*
New York: W. W. Norton, 2010.

Stigler, George. "The University in Political and Social Movements." George
Stigler Papers, Box 22, File 67:04, University of Chicago Archives.

Stigler, George, Harry Kalven Jr., John Hope Franklin, Gwin J. Kolb, Jacob
Getzels, Julian Goldsmith, and Gilbert F. White. "Kalven Committee:
Report on the University's Role in Political and Social Action." University of Chicago, November 11, 1967. http://www-news.uchicago.edu/
releases/07/pdf/kalverpt.pdf.

Stone, Lawrence. "Princeton's Roots: An Amalgam of Models." *Princeton Alumni Weekly*, September 12, 1977. Reprinted in *The Best of PAW*, 2–7.

Thamel, Pete. "Report Faults Binghamton's Leaders in Basketball Scandal." *New York Times*, February 11, 2010. http://www.nytimes.com/2010/02/12/sports/ncaabasketball/12binghamton.html.

"Transcript: Obama's Notre Dame Speech." *Chicago Tribune*, May 17, 2009.

Viner, Jacob. "A Modest Proposal for Some Stress on Scholarship in Graduate Training." Address before the Graduate Convocation, Brown University, June 3, 1950. Brown University Papers XXIV, 1950.

Wilson, Duff. "Facing Sanction, Duke Prosecutor Plans to Resign." *New York Times*, June 16, 2007. http://www.nytimes.com/2007/06/16/us/16duke.html.

———. "Prosecutor in Duke Case Disbarred by Ethics Panel." *New York Times*, June 17, 2007. http://www.nytimes.com/2007/06/17/us/17duke.html.

Wilson, Duff, and David Barstow. "All Charges Dropped in Duke Case." *New York Times*, April 12, 2007. http://www.nytimes.com/2007/04/12/us/12duke.html.

Wilson, Woodrow. *Selected Addresses and Public Papers of Woodrow Wilson*. Edited by Albert Bushnell Hart. Honolulu: University Press of the Pacific, 2002.

Legal Citations

Affidavit of William G. Bowen, Civil Action No. 91-CV-3274, U.S. District Court for the Eastern District of Pennsylvania, April 29, 1992.

Grutter v. Bollinger et al., 539 U.S. 306 (2003).

INDEX